WHERE
IS GOD
in a
MESSED-UP
WORLD?

Roger Carswell

This edition published in Great Britain in 2020

This is a revised and expanded edition of a book with the same title previously
published in 2009 by IVP.

British Library Cataloguing in Publication Data
A record for this book is available from the British Library

ISBN: 978-1-913278-76-2

Designed by Pete Barnsley (CreativeHoot.com)
Printed in Denmark by Nørhaven

10Publishing, a division of 10ofthose.com
Unit C, Tomlinson Road, Leyland, PR25 2DY, England

Email: info@10ofthose.com
Website: www.10ofthose.com

3 5 7 10 8 6 4 2

This book is dedicated to those individuals who were born deaf. They are one of the West's most neglected group of individuals. They may never have heard the birds sing, the enthusiastic chatter of a group of friends or a Beethoven symphony, but I pray that they will hear the still, small voice of Almighty God speaking to their hearts.

You have allowed me to suffer much hardship,
  But You will restore me to life again
  and lift me up from the depths of the earth.
You will restore me to even greater honour
  and comfort me once again.

Psalm 71: 20–21 (NLT)

CONTENTS

Appendices

ACKNOWLEDGEMENTS

Thank you to my wife and friend, Dot, who has demonstrated on a daily basis the strength and confidence that God gives in the face of injustice, suffering, pain and family struggles. I love her, admire her and thank God for her.

Thank you to friends who have shared their own personal struggles, and helped to keep a human, personal perspective when considering the issue of suffering.

I also learned much from my travels to the Middle East, India, and Central and South America. The dire poverty and sense of injustice, particularly when compared to the wealth and indulgence I have witnessed in Europe and the USA, have shaken me to the core.

While I have not suffered to the extent of many, a dark period of depression took me to the depths, and I thank God for all He taught me during this time.

I am also grateful to the hundreds of individuals with whom I have discussed and debated the issues covered in this book. Their genuine questions provided the basis for it.

Finally, my thanks to 10ofthose, and particularly to my editors Emma Balch, who has used her skills to immensely improve what appears in this book, and Eleanor Trotter, for her encouragement and patience in getting the earlier edition of this book to where it is today. Thank you as well to Julie Hatherall and Brian Webster.

PREFACE

I first witnessed a shanty town when I was thirteen. Having been brought up in England, nothing could have prepared me for the shock of seeing such dire poverty and destitution in the Middle East.

Years later, the memory of that first shock gripped me again while working in India and then in Nicaragua. I was deeply stirred by the empty faces and staring eyes of those living off the scraps of rubbish tips, trying to beat dogs and birds to getting anything to eat. A week before I arrived in Nicaragua, in the town next to where I was working, eleven people in one house were discovered, having starved to death. It left me very sombre throughout my time there.

I would love to make, as some say, poverty history. I long for the day when suffering and tears are banished forever. As an ordinary individual, I feel something of the hurt and pain of those who really do experience tragedy and trauma. I have wrestled with issues as to why, and this book is an attempt to answer these big questions. I am as certain that there is a God who creates and cares as I am that this world is not as God designed it.

Roger Carswell, May 2020

INTRODUCTION:
LOOKING FOR GOD IN
A MESSED-UP WORLD

The Students Union bar is packed. Chairs, sofas and floor space are taken up, and it's standing room only. Students tuck into baked potatoes and listen intently. The floor is opened up and they start firing questions:

> *I stopped believing in God when my best friend was killed last year. You say God is loving but if that's true, why would He allow that to happen?*

> *If God is so powerful, why couldn't He stop a tsunami from happening?*

I spend a lot of time visiting universities and colleges, churches and youth events, and everywhere I go I meet people who ask these kinds of questions. For many, their life experience to date may not have brought much personal tragedy. Yet when meeting people of an older generation, I find that they have the same questions but often weighed down with heaviness of heart or a sense of despair at the state of the world. The subject of suffering – and more specifically, why God can't stop wars, pain, death, tragedy, disaster and pandemics – is without a doubt *the* issue people struggle with when it comes to Christianity. And I can understand why.

The issue came into focus again in 2020 when the coronavirus (Covid-19) shook the world. Of course, there have been plagues and pandemics before,[1] but somewhat smugly most of us thought that these were confined to history. With medical advances such as we have, we assumed we could never be impacted in the way that past generations have been.

I have given my life to sharing with others the truth about Jesus Christ and the hope He brings. I believe the Christian gospel (or good news) to be absolutely true. However, at times I have to admit that I too wonder why God does not intervene and stop the human suffering which is so evident in the world around us. I am deeply distressed when I hear of hundreds killed in a train crash in north India; of a baby born with a serious disability; of genocides, war and resulting starvation; of beautiful, little or even unborn children murdered at the hands of the callous and cruel; or the death of a child through cancer.

I don't have an answer for all the 'whys' that I ask, and which people often ask me. But I do have absolute confidence in the character of God and His words to humankind as expressed in the Bible. I have studied what the Bible says about God, and I have seen His transforming power in my life and that of others. As a result, I am convinced that we do have an explanation for why the world is as it is; about why God doesn't put an immediate end to all that is wrong with the world; and that we can find comfort and hope in Him. Christians don't have to be silent on the subject of suffering, even though we cannot explain every individual situation or why one person suffers so much more than another.

The first section of this book looks at the question, 'why?' It considers some of the reasons behind our questions, the places we search for answers and whether we can ultimately find the responses for which we are looking.

The second section focuses on what Christians believe about why the world is as it is. It explains how God intended the world to be, what has gone wrong and what He has – and is – doing about it. The challenge here is to work out whether what the Bible says is true. Are Christians deluded, or not? Is the Bible worth further investigation? Can you share the same certainty as Christians that God *is* in control, and isn't silent?

The third section of the book is more pragmatic and considers how the Christian faith works in practice. It looks, for example, at dealing with pain; the benefits that can come out of tragedy; and how to avoid bitterness and to find comfort.

You may be sceptical about God and how He can speak into all that is wrong with the world. I am also aware that your reason for picking up this book may be because you are carrying deep hurt and raw pain. Please forgive me if at any point I sound glib. It's tough to write generally on a subject which is often deeply personal. I don't claim to be an expert, but I am sure that you can find hope, certainty and answers.

SECTION ONE

CHAPTER 1

LIVING WITH QUESTIONS

A UNIVERSAL PARADOX

John Diamond, Jean-Dominique Bauby and Ivan Noble are each names now famed for writing about their struggle with terminal illness. John Diamond was working as a journalist for *The Times* when he was diagnosed with throat cancer. He eloquently described his journey towards death in a weekly column for the paper. Jean-Dominique Bauby, previously editor-in-chief of the French magazine *Elle*, was paralysed from a stroke. His autobiographical account, *The Diving-Bell and the Butterfly*,[1] which was dictated by 'blinking', captures his claustrophobic struggle with paralysis. It sold over 150,000 copies in the first week of publication. Ivan Noble, a young BBC journalist, chronicled his battle with terminal cancer on the BBC website, which is now published in the book *Like a Hole in the Head*.[2]

Perhaps following the final journal of a dying man appears somewhat strange, a little too voyeuristic. The flood of comments received by the BBC when Noble announced he was too ill to continue the online journal suggest otherwise. People from around the globe sent in their words of appreciation. Many had read each journal entry submitted over three years and thanked Noble for giving them perspective, hope, comfort and inspiration. They were moved by his story of bravery and courage, and how it had made them determined to make more of life, or cope with their own suffering.

Similarly, *The Diving-Bell and the Butterfly* has inspired thousands of readers to appreciate the tragedies (diving-bell) and the joys (butterfly) of life. Perhaps the popularity of his book is due to Bauby's success in capturing this paradox that we each live with on a daily basis. Not all of us can relate to the deep pain of personal tragedy, but we do see and read news of natural disasters, conflict, poverty, suffering and tragic loss of life. We have all experienced some form of disappointment, injustice, pain or tragedy. Yet we also have things to celebrate – things that amaze us, catch us by surprise, warm our heart or put a smile on our face. Sometimes it is the very thing that hurts us that also causes us to experience joy. Certainly Bauby, from his hospital bed, appreciated anew the wonder of life that most of us take for granted – alphabet letters, the taste of 'a simple soft-boiled egg with fingers of toast and lightly salted butter',[3] and the sound of 'blessed silence'.[4]

This tension of the good and the bad, the things we celebrate and those we mourn, is a universal experience. No place or culture on earth is free from it. Young people die in remote communities in Tibet in the same way as they do in Mexico City; train crashes have killed people in India as they have in Japan; children have been murdered indiscriminately in Tasmania, in Scotland and in the USA; thousands have been victims of massive natural disasters from Indonesia to Nicaragua or Armenia.

ASKING THE QUESTION, 'WHY?'

One in ten of the world's population live in extreme poverty. 15,000 children die every day before their fifth birthday, mostly from preventable diseases. The Syrian civil war has cost around half a million deaths and the war in Yemen around 100,000 deaths, and resulted in millions of displaced people and widespread famine. The natural response to statistics like this is: *why?*

On 26 December 2004, a massive earthquake ripped apart the seabed off the coast of Sumatra, causing the world's worst-ever tsunami. It claimed over 300,000 lives and had devastating effects in Indonesia, the Maldives, India, Sri Lanka and Somalia among others. The immediate and long-term impact of such a huge-scale tragedy is hard to comprehend. Again it begs the question: *why?*

Hardly hitting the headlines, due to the extensive worldwide coverage of the tsunami, the Argentine capital of Buenos Aires faced a tragedy of its own just a few days later. Almost 200 young people were killed in a fire that swept through a nightclub in a poor district of the city on 30 December. The death toll almost seemed insignificant in comparison to the tens of thousands being reported dead in Asia the same week, but demonstrations in the streets of Buenos Aires were fuelled by the same question: *why?*

NO-ONE IS IMMUNE

For those of us who have not experienced tragedy on a personal level, we can remain complacent, watching and hearing of war and disaster far from home. We are privileged enough to have confidence in our health services – or at least our emergency services – to rescue us, and are fairly optimistic that we will be accident- or disease-free. We can feel emotion when we see images of children dying of starvation, but we then turn off the TV and tuck into a curry.

Thornton Wilder, a North American novelist and playwright, cut into such smugness in his book *The Bridge of San Luis Rey*. In this deceptively simple book, he unwraps the complex thoughts of those who narrowly missed death in a tragic accident. On 20 July 1714, Wilder explains, 'the finest bridge in all Peru'[5] collapsed. Five travellers plunged to their death, causing all those who had previously crossed the bridge to question their evidently misplaced confidence:

The bridge seemed to be among the things that would last forever; it was unthinkable that it should break.

14

*The moment a Peruvian heard of the accident he signed
himself [with the cross] and made a mental calculation as
to how recently he had crossed by it and how soon he had
intended crossing by it again. People wandered about in
a trance-like state, muttering: they had the hallucination
of seeing themselves falling into a gulf.*[6]

Whether we are victims or perpetrators, everyone is
affected by injustice, evil, disease, disaster or death.
Suffering is inescapable. In ancient times, Job, whose story
is featured in the Bible, mused that just as sparks fly if two
flints are hit together, so human beings eventually suffer.
Death comes to all, but so does sadness, heartache and
pain. We can avoid struggle and confrontation for a while,
but eventually it affects us individually.

My eldest son works with students in New Zealand.
Twice I have visited that beautiful country. The first time
I visited Christchurch, I remember entering the cathedral
and admiring the city. The second time I visited, the city
had been devastated by a dreadful earthquake.[7] I visited the
now temporary, cardboard cathedral, then stood where
once there was a Baptist church building, but now simply
185 white chairs commemorating each person who had
been killed. That was a natural disaster … but then just
eight years later, Australian Brenton Tarrant used a semi-
automatic machine gun to kill fifty-one people gathering
for Friday prayers.[8] This time, untold suffering was the
result of human wickedness.

AN ANCIENT QUESTION

Though the question *'why?'* is substantial, it is not new. It is raised in the Book of Job, the oldest book within the Bible. The protagonist, Job, lost everything in a matter of days. His sons and daughters were killed, his business collapsed and he lost his health. He asked, *'why?'* – and who can blame him? He desperately sought answers, and not always in the right places, but he wanted to understand his own predicament. Years later, one of the Bible's most powerful preachers, Habakkuk, asked God the same question when his country was invaded by the barbarous Babylonians. Although he accepted that his people had been far from virtuous, Habakkuk couldn't understand how things would be better under the rule of a nation which was notorious for its torturous and wicked ways.

The Bible has many heroes, and some great characters, but its focal person is Jesus. It anticipates His coming to earth, then describes His life and work, before applying the effect of His accomplishments to a fledgling church and Christian believers of all time. Yet Jesus has been described as the 'suffering servant';[9] God Himself identifies with the sorrows and heartache of the world. For two thousand years, those who have trusted and followed Jesus have been a people who have suffered through persecution, poverty and derision, as well as the ordinary trials of life.

Using images and pictures to convey the depth of their hurt, various Bible authors describe in distilled emotion their experiences. It is like being in a furnace,[10] or in a storm,[11] or in warfare,[12] or like experiencing travail and giving birth,[13] or being threshed after harvest,[14] or running a race,[15] or enduring a judicial trial.[16]

Attempts to provide answers to the question *'why?'* are many, but few are satisfactory. After all, if there is a God and we are part of His creation, who are we to understand His ways? If God is God, then surely He can do as He wishes. He is always going to be beyond our comprehension. We read in the Bible that God says, 'For My thoughts are not your thoughts, nor are your ways My ways.'[17] On the other hand, surely it is right to use the enquiring mind that God has given us to search out and wrestle with issues such as: 'Why doesn't God stop the injustice, wars and poverty in the world?'; 'If He doesn't intervene, is He really a God of love?'; as well as 'What is the meaning of *my* suffering?'

CHAPTER 2

LOOKING FOR ANSWERS

TWO REALITIES

Never shall I forget that night, the first night in camp, which has turned my life into one long night, seven times cursed and seven times sealed. Never shall I forget that smoke. Never shall I forget the little faces of the children, whose bodies I saw turned into wreaths of smoke beneath a silent blue sky.

Never shall I forget those flames which consumed my faith forever.

Never shall I forget that nocturnal silence which deprived me, for all eternity, of the desire to live. Never shall I forget those moments, which murdered my God and my soul and turned my dreams to dust. Never shall I forget these things, even if I am condemned to live as long as God himself. Never.[1]

These words were penned by Nobel Peace Prize winner Elie Wiesel, describing his first night of captivity at Auschwitz concentration camp. He was born in Sighet, Transylvania in 1928 to a Jewish family. Both his parents and his younger sister were killed in the extermination camps, but he survived and later became Professor in Humanities at Boston University, as well as a prolific writer.

The writings of Elie Wiesel are powerful prose, but there is intrigue too. Wiesel combines his certainty that God is real with a temporary loss of faith in God because of the horrendous suffering that he witnessed. Later in life, as a Jew, he wrote with confidence about his belief in God. I can relate to Wiesel's sentiments. I have not experienced suffering like he did as a young boy, but like him I wrestle with the two realities of God being God and the world being as it is.

WANTING IT BOTH WAYS

Whether we like to admit it or not, our world is characterised by suffering and evil. There is something like a seed within us that grows and which permeates every part of our being, leading us to do wrong. However, we also recognise that we should not be like this. It is not that God is playing games with us. We have turned our backs on God and His ways, and inevitably suffer the consequences. Some of us want to know God, but we all want to do our own thing. We don't like God to control us, but we would prefer to live without suffering the consequence of a world in rebellion against Him.

Despite our marginalising God, we still want Him to be accountable to standards of what we believe to be fair, just, loving and helpful to us. So when trouble strikes, we ask: 'Why doesn't God act in a decisive way?' 'Where is He in the maze of human existence?' The Greek philosopher, Epicurus, outlined the dilemma facing the thinking mind:

> God either wishes to take away evils and is unable; or He is able and is unwilling; or He is neither willing nor able; or He is both willing and able. If He is willing but unable, He is feeble, which is not in accordance with the character of God. If He is able and unwilling, He is envious, which is equally at variance with God. If He is neither willing nor able, He is both envious and feeble, and therefore not God. If He is both willing and able, which alone is suitable for God, from what source then are evils? Or why does He not remove them?[2]

Two millennia later, the English novelist and poet Thomas Hardy found himself facing similar questions. In the unsatisfactory state of having basic, unanswered questions, but fearing that God is either impotent or cruel, he wrote the poem 'Nature's Questioning':

> We wonder, we wonder, why we find us here!
> Has some Vast Imbecility,

Mighty to build and blend,
But impotent to tend,
Framed us in jest, and left us now to hazardry?[3]

A SPIRITUAL DIMENSION

All of this assumes a belief in a personal God. There is within every human being an awareness of something 'Other'. There is a spiritual dimension, an incurably religious bent deep inside the psyche of us all. This consciousness of something or someone greater than ourselves leads us to pray, to ask bewildering questions or to blame someone other than ourselves. Such a conclusion is based on an inflated view of our own ability to reach watertight conclusions, and on a defective conclusion which assumes we have exhausted all the possibilities of what God could be like. Others simply dismiss belief in God, but in doing so confine themselves to the belief that life is a meaningless cul-de-sac. They take a giant 'step of faith' in saying that there is no designer behind the design, no maker behind the things made and no creator behind creation. Though Richard Dawkins and Jacques Derrida argue for life being meaningless from a scientific and philosophical perspective respectively, there is something unacceptable and unconvincing about what they say. For them, a piece of paper, for example, has more meaning than a human being, because at least it was manufactured for a purpose, unlike men and women.

Significantly, the vocal atheistic lobby – who regularly appear in the media with their notion of survival of the fittest and their horrible notion that epidemics are simply 'mother earth thinning its ranks' – were not found in the media studios during the coronavirus pandemic. Whatever they may have said, life is not 'just dancing to one's DNA'. That did not ring true when people were facing fear and death. We know that actually life is very precious.

There is a host of atheists that the media regularly promote, who are in a weak place if asked to give comfort in a situation of suffering. It is cheap to pour scorn on those who look to God for answers. Read again Richard Dawkins' infamous words and ask whether they help the hungry, the sick, the grieving, the fearful, the dying, or if they are callous conclusions of a doctrine that comforts the self-righteous, materialism of the West.

> *In a universe of electrons and selfish genes, blind forces and genetic replication, some people are going to get hurt, other people are going to get lucky, and you won't find any rhyme or reason in it, nor any justice. The universe that we observe has precisely the properties we should expect if there is, at bottom, no design, no purpose, no evil, no good, nothing but blind, pitiless indifference. DNA neither knows nor cares. DNA just is. And we dance to its music.*[4]

A GREAT DECEPTION

It is a tragic thing to be deceived or deluded by our own imaginations. The problem with being deceived is that we never realise that we are deceived. The autobiography of Sir Alec Guinness, *Blessings in Disguise*, tells about an incident when he was playing Father Brown on location in Burgundy. Walking back to his lodgings one evening, still wearing his priest's costume, it grew dark:

> *I hadn't gone far when I heard scampering footsteps and a piping voice calling, 'Mon Père!' My hand was seized by a boy of seven or eight, who clutched it tightly, swung it and kept up a non-stop prattle … Although I was a total stranger he obviously took me for a priest and so to be trusted. Suddenly, with a 'Bonsoir Mon Père', and a hurried sideways sort of bow, he disappeared through a hole in the hedge. He had a happy, reassuring walk home, and I was left with an odd calm sense of elation …*[5]

There were two happy individuals, but their contentment was based on delusion. To keep God at a distance and to live as if He were dead or irrelevant may be the politically correct or socially acceptable thing to do. However, not only does it leave plenty of unanswered questions, it is self-delusion because God has revealed Himself to us. He has done so in several ways, but principally through Jesus Christ and the Bible.[6]

A GOD WHO IS

Basic to Christian belief is the conviction that God has revealed Himself to humanity. We have all heard someone say, 'Well, my view of God is …' The problem with following such philosophising is that there would be billions of individual ideas about God. The Bible says that human beings were made in God's image, which was quite a compliment! It is an insult to God, though, if we try to make *Him* in our image. When the question, 'Why doesn't God stop everything that's wrong with the world?' is asked, assumptions are being made about the character of God. These may be true, but we have to be careful that the God we are questioning isn't one we have invented. It would be foolish to have a god of our own devising, who subsequently doesn't quite fit into all we would have imagined of him, and so dismiss the notion of a deity and regard ourselves as non-believers. I have often asked atheists the simple question, 'What sort of a god don't you believe in?' Having listened to their answer, I reply that I too would be an atheist if that is what God is like.

WHAT GOD IS LIKE

The Bible teaches that God is a spirit, who has all power, is all-knowing and is everywhere. He never changes, and is totally just and infinitely loving. God is good. He is bigger than, and beyond, all things, and yet interested and involved in the details of the things that concern us. As God, He does not *have* to explain Himself to us. And yet He has made Himself known to us.

As we read the words of Jesus, and the Bible as a whole, we learn that there is only one God. God is a triune God, who is Father, Son and Holy Spirit; three Persons in one God, yet one God in three Persons. God is personal, hence our calling God 'Him'. It is not that God has gender, but that He has personality. He feels and experiences emotions. Time and again in the Bible, we read that God is altogether wise, knowing and powerful. Paul, one of the main contributors to the New Testament part of the Bible, wrote, 'Oh, the depth of the riches both of the wisdom and knowledge of God! How unsearchable are His judgments, and His ways past finding out! "For who has known the mind of the Lord? Or who has become His counsellor?"'[7]

The Bible makes it clear that God is altogether loving, patient and compassionate. The familiar words of the Bible that 'God is love'[8] are revolutionary as far as millions of devotees of different religions are concerned. Unlike their gods, the God of the Bible is not capricious, spiteful, unpredictable and nasty. He is absolutely pure, loving and just. The Bible repeatedly teaches this, for example: 'Righteousness and justice are the foundation of Your throne; Mercy and truth go before Your face.'[9] And: 'Great and marvellous are [Your] deeds, Lord God Almighty. Just and true are [Your] ways, King of the ages.'[10]

MYSTERY AND CERTAINTY

All that we know about God is because of what He has revealed to us, and yet we do not understand all things. We only know in part, and cannot put all the cogs of God's working together. This twin truth of mystery and certainty is the key to answering the question of *'why?'*

26

In the Book of Deuteronomy in the Bible, we read, 'The secret things belong to the Lord our God, but the things revealed belong to us and to our children for ever, that we may follow all the words of this law.'[11]

If we could comprehend everything there was to understand about God, either He would not be God, or we would not be mere humans. Our finite, frail and often fickle minds are never going to fathom the depths of an infinite and eternal God.

There are things we will never be able to understand or explain. There are concepts and incidents that are beyond us. Christians believe that God is wise in His reservations as well as His revelations. Despite all the unanswered questions and bewildering issues of life, we have the solid character of God who is totally reliable. There will always be a sense in which the Christian will be agnostic: we do not know or understand things as God does. Yet we have a firm confidence that God knows what He is doing and always does what is best. Matthew Henry observed, 'The God of Israel, the Saviour, is sometimes a God that hides Himself, but never a God that absents Himself; sometimes in the dark, but never at a distance.'[12] There are countless promises in the Bible in which the Christian rests, which give this assurance. If some people see these as a crutch, perhaps there is some truth in that thought, but then crutches can be very helpful to those who are injured!

Christian confidence and certainty, even in times of great suffering, is based not on an explanation from God as to why, but on the assurance of God's purpose and presence. When Verna Wright, the eminent Professor of Rheumatology in Leeds University, was struggling with cancer, he experienced great comfort from the knowledge that God was in control, even though he himself may not have chosen the path allotted to him. Wanting to comfort his daughter who also had cancer, he quoted the words of a hymn:

I am not skilled to understand
What God has willed,
What God has planned;
I only know at his right hand
Stands one who is my Saviour.[13]

Helen Roseveare, a missionary doctor, faced this same tension between mystery and certainty, between the secret things and the revealed things. She studied medicine at Cambridge University, where she became a Christian, through friends in the Christian Union. Eventually she went to the Belgian Congo (Democratic Republic of the Congo) to work as a missionary doctor. She personally supervised the building of several hospitals, and did a remarkable work not only in caring for patients but in training doctors and nurses.

During the Belgian Congo uprising in 1964, she was captured by Zimba rebels. Brutalised, raped and imprisoned, she was taken out of prison to be shot. She was miraculously granted a reprieve, and eventually escaped the Congo and returned to her home in Northern

Ireland. When the uprising came to an end, despite all her ordeals, she went back to continue her work in the Congo. Naturally, there were huge physical and emotional scars, but reflecting on what had happened, she said, 'I came to the conclusion that I could ask myself the question: "Can I thank God that He trusts me with this suffering even if He never tells me why?"'[14]

As Christians, we are encouraged to call God, 'Father'. He is a personal God. Although we do not understand all things, we enjoy a relationship with God, which is intimate and real. It is like a husband–wife relationship, or that of a parent and child. And as a child has trust in his or her father (though sadly, sometimes, this is a misplaced trust), likewise we, as believers, are confident that God knows best. The Bible gives us what is in effect a family secret: 'And we know that all things work together for good to those who love God, to those who are the called according to His purpose.'[15] We are not God, so we do not know everything, but we can trust in, and have a relationship with, God who does know and is in control.[16] We are not able to give an array of explanations to each individual's suffering, but God has revealed to us principles which leave clues, which may in turn help us to explain. As the prolific North American author Warren Wiersbe put it, 'People live by promises and not by explanations.' That is the basis for this famous quotation: 'All I have seen teaches me to trust the Creator for all I have not seen.'[17] Trusting that God knows best, even if we cannot fathom the intricacies of what is happening, leads to a position where one can trust and feel at peace knowing that God is in control of all things.

Habakkuk lived as a prophet in about 600 bc. He complained to God that His people were being so badly abused by the Babylonians, and could not understand God's apparent silence. God answered Habakkuk, and turned his complaining into prayer and confidence in God, even if life was still 'unbearable'. Habakkuk's prophecy in the Bible ends with an upbeat song affirming his joy in God:

> *Though the fig-tree does not bud*
> *   and there are no grapes on the vines,*
> *though the olive crop fails*
> *   and the fields produce no food,*
> *though there are no sheep in the sheepfold*
> *   and no cattle in the stalls,*
> *yet I will rejoice in the Lord,*
> *   I will be joyful in God my Saviour.*[18]

SECTION TWO

CHAPTER 3

THE WORLD AS IT WAS

A WORLD AWAY FROM OURS

The first book of the Bible, the Book of Genesis, is the book of beginnings: the beginning of the universe, of the planet earth, of life, of the human race, of language, of family life, of civilisation, of nations, of government. It also has the beginning of sin, suffering and death, and the beginning of the promise of forgiveness and reconciliation to God.

The opening, dramatic pages of the Bible portray a world very different from our own. In Genesis chapter 1, we read how day after day God is creating, and at the climax of each day pronouncing all that He has brought into being as 'good'. On the sixth day, when He made man and woman, God went further and then pronounced creation as 'very good'. So humans, with our desires, drives, emotions and personalities, were seen by our Maker as perfect. The paradise, which God had created on earth, had no sin, suffering, sickness, sadness or death. There was no struggle for existence, no cruelty, no pollution and no physical calamities, such as floods, earthquakes, pandemics, hurricanes or tsunamis; there was no imbalance – in order or justice. Rather, the first humans lived their lives as companions and lovers, with nothing to hide from each other or God. They enjoyed God's presence with them, and He delighted in them. Harmony existed between heaven and earth. There was freedom, purity, security, love, trust and peace; concepts such as guilt, fear, evil, lust, selfishness, revenge and bitterness were alien to this world. If all this seems like a fairy tale, surely it is because we have become so distant from what God originally intended.

John Milton tried to describe how the world was and what Adam felt at the beginning of time. Here are the words Milton put in Adam's mouth as he spoke to the archangel Raphael:

> Hill, dale, and shady woods, and sunny plains,
> And liquid lapse of murmuring streams; by these,
> Creatures that live, and moved, and walked, or flew;
> Birds on the branches warbling; all things smiled.[1]

The Bible never seeks to prove the existence of God; it assumes it. The Book of Genesis, and therefore the Bible, opens with the words, 'In the beginning God created the heavens and the earth.'[2] These words were read to a listening world by the crew of the Apollo 8 at

Christmas 1968, after they had become the first humans to circumnavigate the moon. This sentence alone refutes atheism, pantheism, polytheism, humanism and materialism. Deism, the belief that God has made the world and left it to its own devices, is also discredited in the unfolding drama of the Book of Genesis. Rather, the Bible teaches that God is intimately involved in all the details of our world, and each individual within it.

Of course, it can be argued that as God knows everything, He would have known what would happen and He could have taken preventative measures. Why would God create an order that would become flawed and be the cause of so much human misery? Certainly God is not confined to or limited by time or space; the past, present and future are all known to God. In fact, the Bible speaks of Jesus and His crucifixion as, '… the Lamb who was slain from the creation of the world.'[3] Clearly, when the first human beings dared to defy God, shaking their fist in His face and rebelling against His explicit command, God was not taken by surprise. There was no emergency cabinet meeting in heaven desperately trying to sort out a solution to the problem. In what we can only call the wisdom of God, He knew what was to happen and did not remove our ability to disobey Him.

Professor John Lennox is very helpful here, saying that we should distinguish:

> … *between God's permissive will – the fact that God created a universe in which evil is possible –and God's*

directive will – those thing which God actively does. The
New Testament is clear that God is never the author of
evil – so it is possible in the world that He made, but
it is not His intention for the world that He has made.
That is to say, human beings have a certain amount of
independence that allows things to go wrong. Richard
Dawkins and Stephen Hawking thought that we live in a
deterministic universe. We do not.[4]

The Bible says, 'Let no one say when he is tempted, "I am tempted by God"; for God cannot be tempted by evil, nor does He Himself tempt anyone.'[5]

Without tying up all the ends, 1700 years ago Augustine expressed what Christians believe today: 'God judged it better to bring good out of evil than to suffer no evil to exist.'[6] There is a sense in which I am content to leave it there, as any attempt to explain the machinations of God's infinite mind would be speculative. I dare not go beyond what God has revealed to us about Himself. To do so would be to start to create my own god.

A WONDERFUL WORLD?

Despite all the wickedness and suffering in the world, there is still great beauty, kindness, loveliness, awe and wonder. They are all remnants of all that is and which characterised the world that God made. Our emotions are stirred when we hear one of the greatest jazz musicians of all time, Louis Armstrong, sing the now classic 'What a Wonderful World':

The colours of the rainbow so pretty in the sky
Are also on the faces of people going by
I see friends shaking hands saying how do you do
They're really saying 'I love you'.

I hear babies crying, I watch them grow
They'll learn much more than I'll ever know
And I think to myself, what a wonderful world
Yes, I think to myself, what a wonderful world.[7]

While we recognise that the world is marred, like Louis Armstrong, we see that it is also majestic. One of the distinguishing features of modern life is that we are bombarded with countless images of the horrors taking place around the world. Even Armstrong's song of celebration was set against the indescribable horrors of the Vietnam War in the 1987 film *Good Morning, Vietnam*. Images of atrocities are so commonplace on our TV screens and in our newspapers that our perception of reality can be eroded by the daily barrage of so constant a flow of such images. The danger then exists that we can become duplicitous, having the apparent ability to show great sympathy and even compassion one minute, and a little later to live as if there are no cares in the world.

Leslie Davis – a North American journalist and Foreign Service officer who worked in Turkey and Armenia at the beginning of the twentieth century – recognised this ability to follow Lord Nelson's example in raising a telescope to a blind eye. At first Davis wrote about 'how peacefully the Armenians and Turks were getting along'[8]. But not long after he would write about the genocide of the Armenian people, 'Who could have then foreseen, amid these peaceful surroundings, that the following year there was to be in this region what is probably the most terrible tragedy that has befallen any people in the history of the world?'[9] He described one of the perpetrators of the genocide, Sabit Bey, as having something sociopathic about his behaviour:

> I have seen tears roll down the cheeks of him at the imaginary sufferings of a young man who was playing the part of a wounded soldier in an amateur theatrical performance given for the benefit of the Turkish Red Crescent Society. Yet a hundred thousand people were made homeless and most of them perished from violence as a result of his orders.[10]

There is sometimes an act of kindness or sensitivity from even the most evil of men. One thinks how different they would be if only their true character, which God had created, had not been hijacked by the cruel understudy of sin. It is all too easy to express horror at the suffering and injustice in the world, and yet contribute to the wrongs of our world by selfish living, pretending that the world revolves around us. There is something great about each human being, but also something absolutely awful.

CASE STUDY 1

NAME: Dave and Jan

SITUATION: Married couple with four young children, two of whom have a rare degenerative disease

Dave and Jan met at university, where Dave was studying engineering and Jan medicine. During their first year of studies, through different circumstances, they had become Christians. They both realised that they had a problem of wrong within themselves and that their most pressing need was to respond to God's love for 'sinners', expressed through the death of Jesus Christ on the cross. Becoming Christians made a huge difference to them as they experienced God's forgiveness in their lives. They began to read the Bible and see its relevance to their lives. Not long after graduation, they were married and set up home.

They had four children within five years. Hannah was first, followed closely by Amy, Josh and finally Daniel. At first, things seemed as normal as they could be with young children in the home, but when Amy was about three, Dave and Jan began to realise that her development was different from that of her older sister, Hannah. She appeared to be hyperactive, had continual ear problems and never slept through the night. She would often wake up, sometimes ten times a night, and then really struggle to get back to sleep. 'Although things didn't seem quite right,' they explain, 'we were not particularly concerned, as we had no idea of the underlying problem.'

Amy eventually started nursery school and then moved up into reception class at school. She was always affectionate and very popular with both pupils and teachers alike. It was during this year that her problems became more noticeable as she started to fall further behind her peers at school. She could barely put a few words together, would only scribble and did not concentrate on the tasks she was given to do.

During this year, Dave and Jan were referred to a local paediatrician. They suspect that he realised what the problem was as soon as he saw Amy, but over the next few months he carried out various tests on all the family. Samples were sent off to Great Ormond Street Hospital for children for analysis. During one of their appointments, he hinted that he thought the problem was a rare genetic disorder and said that he was awaiting confirmation.

During the weeks that followed, life continued relatively normally, but gradually Jan started to believe that there was something seriously wrong. And so began the rollercoaster emotions of facing the fact that Amy would not have a 'normal' life. As a Christian, Jan believed that God was in control, but the pain was still real.

At a later appointment with the paediatrician, he confirmed what was suspected: Amy had Sanfilippo syndrome – MPS (mucopolysaccharide) Type III(b) – one of a family of rare genetic disorders. Not only did Amy, who was nearly six, have Sanfilippo syndrome, but Daniel, who was almost three, had the same disease. Jan looked in her medical textbooks to find out more about the condition, but there was very limited information as the condition was so rare. Over the next few days, they learnt more about the implications of Sanfilippo on the lives of Amy and Daniel. The paediatrician, trying to break the news gently, called at their house the following evening with a leaflet from the MPS Society, a national support group, telling more about what to expect in the future.

The life of a child with Sanfilippo can generally be divided into three phases. The first few years appear as fairly normal development. In the following years, they become extremely hyperactive, but development levels off and they do not acquire the skills expected. The final stage is a degenerative phase where they slow down, losing speech, mobility and all other skills. Average life expectancy is around fourteen years.

The days and weeks that followed the diagnosis were not easy. Coming to terms with the fact that two of their four children had a serious problem with a limited life expectancy was tough. Dave and Jan appreciated the support from the MPS Society, who helped them through some of the practical considerations and adjustments that had to be made both then and in the following years. Family and friends were good to them, although they often found it difficult facing up to the shock of what Dave and Jan had already started to go through.

'Through it all there was something else which supported us and kept is going. We were acutely aware of the presence of God in a very real way,' says Dave. 'While at university, we had both come to trust in Christ for the forgiveness of our sin. Since then, He had made a real difference in our lives as we tried, with His help, to walk with Him and live for Him. Now, in the midst of difficult times, we had a great sense of His strengthening and upholding hand upon our lives. Although we couldn't understand why this should happen to us, we found that we were able to trust God fully. We are confident that God does not make mistakes and that, although things can be difficult, He is with us in the difficulties.'

Over the years since Amy and Daniel were first diagnosed with Sanfilippo, they have continued to deteriorate. Amy (now twenty-nine) cannot talk or walk without help. Daniel (now twenty-six) has no speech or mobility. Both of them are totally dependent on others. They cannot make their needs known or feed themselves. They have no idea of the problems that they have. However, both of them are extremely affectionate and continue to be a great joy to Dave, Jan, Hannah and Josh, as well as to others who know them.

Reflecting on their situation, Jan says, 'We have continued to know [God's] help in recent years. It hasn't always been easy, but God has been good. We have had to learn to take one day at a time and to trust God day by day. As we look back, we are overwhelmed by the goodness of God through it all, and as we anticipate difficult days ahead, our trust is in God who hasn't failed us in the past.'

CHAPTER 4

THE WORLD TAKES A TURN

NO LONGER PERFECT

The perfect world, created by God, was to be wrecked and ruined in an instant when the first man and woman deliberately disobeyed God, insisting that they should discover evil. The Bible, which Christians believe to be God's message to humanity, graphically describes this moment,[1] which was to change the face of history and take from us what would have been a very different world order. It led to the first man and woman being expelled from the paradise of the Garden of Eden. Instead, they were to live in a world wrecked and ruined by the catastrophic consequences of sin. Their world would be characterised by a separation from God, as well as suffering and death, bringing disaster to all of creation.

Today, in the material realm, everything has a tendency to wear out and decay. In the living world, animals, as well as humans, are engaged in a constant struggle against disease and predators, and they also are affected by ageing and death. Culturally, civilisations rise for a time and then crumble and die. In the spiritual and moral realm, we find it easier to do wrong than to do right. At several levels, our world is characterised by alienation, and hence is full of hatred, crime, war, pollution, selfishness, injustice and dishonesty. Clearly, something has gone wrong with what was initially perfect.

Although we do not know the ultimate origin of evil, we are told that it was never God's desire that human beings should discover or imbibe it. Outside of Genesis chapter 3 there is no explanation that makes sense of the mess and muddle which is endemic in our world. The Bible makes it clear that the world we now live in is not as God desired it to be. If incidents of suffering and wrongdoing leave *us* feeling hurt, they affect the loving and compassionate God in a far greater way. Time and again, as God reveals Himself to us in the Bible, He has demonstrated that He really does care, and that His heart is towards us.

AN INTERNAL PROBLEM

The film *The Pianist*, directed and produced by Roman Polanski and starring Adrien Brody, features a Polish Jew, who is an outstanding pianist, on the run from the Nazis. He owes his survival ultimately to a Nazi officer who shows compassion to him. In Wladyslaw Szpilman's autobiographical book which led to the film, we are given extracts from his diary. He makes the point that the origin of the world's atrocities lies in the individual human heart and our defiance against God:

1 September 1942

Why did this war have to happen at all? Because humanity had to be shown where its godlessness was taking it …

There are no commandments now against stealing, killing or lying, not if they go against people's personal interest. This denial of God's commandments leads to all the other immoral manifestations of greed – unjust self-enrichment, hatred, deceit, sexual licence resulting in infertility and the downfall of the German people. God allows all this to happen, lets these forces have power and allows so many innocent people to perish to show mankind that without Him we are only animals in conflict, who believe we have to destroy each other. We will not listen to the divine commandment: 'Love one another'. Very well, then, says God, try the Devil's commandment, the opposite: 'Hate one another'. We know the story of the Deluge from Holy Scripture. Why did the first race of men come to such a tragic end? Because they had abandoned God and must die, guilty and innocent alike. They had only themselves to blame for their punishment. And it is the same today.[2]

INNATELY EVIL

On 20 April1999, in the small, suburban town of Littleon, Colorado in the USA, two intelligent teenage boys from solid homes entered their school in the middle of the day with knives, guns and bombs. They planned to kill hundreds of their peers. By the end of the day, twelve students, one teacher and two murderers, Dylan Klebold and Eric Harris, were dead.

In trying to understand how such a massacre could have happened, many pointed the finger of blame at Dylan's and Eric's parents for failing to bring them up well. Ten years after the event, Dylan's mother, Susan, said in Oprah Winfrey's magazine, 'In raising Dylan, I taught him how to protect himself from a host of dangers: lightening, snake bites, head injuries, skin cancer, smoking, drinking, sexually transmitted diseases, drug addiction, reckless driving, even carbon monoxide poisoning. It never occurred to me that the gravest danger – to him and, as it turned out, to many others – might come from within.'[3]

There are times when we are driven to the conclusion that the wickedness of certain behaviour is beyond rational, human behaviour. For example, Dr Richard Badcock, a psychiatrist at Rampton Special Hospital near Retford, spent more than a hundred hours with Dr Harold Shipman, Britain's worst serial murderer. Shipman had worked as a family doctor in communities where he was trusted. Yet this seemingly inoffensive doctor was repeatedly murdering his patients. Badcock argued that

Shipman was a 'classic necrophiliac', but added, 'Equally you make a case for it being a spiritual disorder. It is a disorder that transcends the conventional disciplines of medicine, psychology and religion. It is something that presumably many could get into but don't. I think evil comes into it.'[4]

However, in some circles to 'behave badly' has become an acceptable, admirable and commendable mode of behaviour. We recognise and repeat that we are all tarred with the same brush and that 'nobody is perfect', but such attitudes are rarely a humble admission that we are not the people we were created to be. By nature, 'all have sinned and fall short of the glory of God'.[5] The Ten Commandments in the Old Testament not only show us what is right behaviour but, like a stethoscope, show us up for being wrong at the very heart of our being. Jesus summarised the Ten Commandments by saying that we should love the Lord our God with all our heart, soul and mind, and that we should love our neighbours as ourselves.[6] Not one of us can claim to have lived in this way.

THE BLAME GAME

When we are proved to be failing in some way, it is tempting to argue that the root cause is somebody else's fault. It is an old ploy; as some wag has said, 'Adam blamed Eve, Eve blamed the serpent, and the serpent hadn't a leg to stand on.' In more recent times, the classic demonstration of this was at the Nuremberg Trials in 1945–46 where the Nazi war criminals were indicted for their crimes against humanity. Josef Seuss, an administrative assistant, whimpered, 'A soldier can only carry out his orders.' Walter Langlesit, a battalion commander, declared, 'I was just a little man. Those things were done on orders from the big shots.' Colonel Hoess, commandant of the notorious Auschwitz concentration camp, who personally supervised the extermination of two and a half million Jews, explained, 'In Germany it was understood that if something went wrong, the man who gave the orders was responsible. So I didn't think I would ever have to answer for it myself.' Hermann Goering, founder of the Gestapo and Luftwaffe, and formerly the second-ranking man in Germany, blustered, 'We had to obey orders.'[7]

In August 2002, Holly Wells and Jessica Chapman – two ten-year-old girls from Soham, Cambridgeshire – were murdered. The crime seemed all the more horrific because the killer was actually a trusted friend known to the girls through school, and living within walking distance of their home. Newspaper columnists wrote articles horrified at what had happened, but assuring their readers that we are not really bad, although once in a while there may be an outburst of wickedness. That is not how the Bible views us. Jesus, speaking about prayer, said, 'If you then, though you are evil …'[8] As a result of what theologians call 'the Fall', when the first human beings rebelled against the authority and will of God, we have inherited a nature which is inherently bad. That does not mean that we can do nothing commendable. We still find joy in being involved in good works, but even they can be spoiled by wrong motives and pride. However, it does mean that we are each capable of disobeying God in ways that may hit the headlines or simply harden our hearts.

God has consistently hated sin; He never grows accustomed to it in the way that we do. By nature, He is absolutely truthful, clean and holy. He is impeccable in His purity, justice and goodness. He is without hypocrisy, duplicity and sham. By nature, He cannot overlook our wrongdoing. How different from us.

Mike Wallace, a North American television interviewer, introduced a programme about the Nazi Adolf Eichmann, a principal architect of the Holocaust. At the outset he posed a central question, 'How is it possible … for a man to act as Eichmann acted? Was he a monster? A madman? Or was he perhaps something more terrifying: was he normal?'

The most startling answer to Wallace's shocking question came in an interview with Yehiel Dinur, a concentration camp survivor who testified against Eichmann at his trial in 1961. A film clip shows Dinur walking into the courtroom, then stopping short after seeing Eichmann for the first time since the Nazi had sent him to Auschwitz eighteen years earlier. Dinur began to sob uncontrollably, then fainted, collapsing in a heap on the floor as the presiding judicial official pounded his gavel for order in the crowded courtroom.

Was Dinur overcome by hatred? Fear? Horrid memories?

No, it was none of these. Rather, as Dinur explained to Wallace, all at once he realised that Eichmann was not the godlike officer who had sent so many to their deaths. This Eichmann was an ordinary man. 'I was afraid about myself,' said Dinur. '… I saw that I am capable to do this. *I am … exactly like he.*'[9]

'Eichmann is in all of us' is a sobering and horrifying thought. To confront evil, as Dinur did, can be a devastating experience. Nevertheless, as one reads the Bible, it is clear that God adamantly wants us to face the reality of who we are and what we are like. It is not that God's intention is to leave us cowering and guilt-ridden, but that He might forgive, transform and free us, making us the people we were created to be.

Warren Wiersbe notes that:

> *There is something worse than suffering, and that is sin. Don't pity Jesus on the cross. Instead, pity Caiaphas, the scheming religious liar; or Pilate, the spineless Roman politician; or Judas, the money-grabbing thief who wasted the opportunity of a lifetime. We shed tears, and rightly so, for a loved one killed in an accident; but too often we don't weep for the drunken driver who caused the accident. We permit our suffering to blind us to the real cause of suffering in this world – human rebellion against God.*[10]

However, that does not necessarily mean that the reason one individual suffers more than another is that he or she has done something particularly bad, and therefore they have 'displeased the gods'. Superstition or muddled religious thinking can sometimes lead a person who has been diagnosed with a serious illness, or is going through particularly difficulty times, to believe they are being punished. However, Jesus firmly dispelled such a notion. In John chapter 9, we read:

> *Now as Jesus passed by, He saw a man who was blind from birth. And His disciples asked Him, saying, 'Rabbi, who sinned, this man or his parents, that he was born blind?'*

> *Jesus answered, 'Neither this man nor his parents sinned, but that the works of God should be revealed in him.'[11]*

Jesus was not teaching that the man born blind and his parents were sinless, for elsewhere He makes it very clear that we are all sinful.[12] The point is that the sinful nature and actions of the man and his parents did not directly lead to the man's blindness. We are all caught up in the bundle of life, and that means that we may well find ourselves suffering or struggling in one way or another. It is the world in which we are living, rather than the things of which we are guilty, that is the cause.

Our world has become a place where evil, injustice and suffering prevail. Blaming individuals or powers does not alleviate the hurt that is felt, nor provide answers as to the cause and cure of what is wrong. To find the source of suffering, though, may help to provide the remedy, relieve the pain and create hope for the future.

CASE STUDY 2

NAMES: Mosey family

SITUATION: John and Lisa lost their daughter in the terrorist attack on Pan Am flight 103, which exploded over Lockerbie, Scotland

John and Lisa Mosey will never forget Christmas1988. It has become the pivot of their lives; the point which separates all the events and memories. As John turned on the TV to catch the news on the evening of 21 December, his immediate emotion was sympathy for the passengers and crew of a plane that crashed over a small Scottish town. Sixteen-year-old Marcus was sitting on the sofa, and Lisa and John were perched on the arm. 'How awful – the poor people!' they remember one of them saying. Then the news reporter continued with the details: 'Pan Am flight 103, flying from London to New York, exploded above the Scottish border at about three minutes past seven, raining its debris down on this little town of Lockerbie.'

'That's Helga's flight,' burst from Lisa's lips. John had returned only a few hours earlier from driving their nineteen-year-old daughter from their home near Birmingham to Heathrow airport. The possibility of such a thing happening to her just hadn't crossed his mind. 'These things happen to others; they never happen to me.' Like many of us, he was used to being just an observer of other people's tragedies. There followed a stunned silence as the unthinkable slowly expanded, filling not only their minds but every nerve and cell of their bodies.

'No! No! No! No!' broke the silence as Marcus screamed at the screen. The solitary word 'Helga ...' quietly, almost silently, managed to escape from somewhere deep down inside Lisa. John stood as if dumb, his tongue unable to articulate. The news flash ended and the news report moved on to other, seemingly trivial, matters, such as how many millions of pounds were being spent that Christmas using credit cards, sport results and the weather forecast.

Helga was a talented musician, accomplished on the piano, recorder and violin, but her real passion was singing. Her mezzo-soprano voice was in demand. She sang with one of the country's leading Bach choirs and was selected from all of the schools in Britain to sing in the National Youth Choir. Her ambition was to sing professionally. A music professor at Lancaster University, where she had secured a place to study music, said that he had little doubt that she would make her mark on the music world.

They switched off the TV. John remembers saying something about asking God to help them. Then the three of them stood together in the middle of the room with their arms around each other as they lifted up their broken and perplexed hearts to God in prayer. Now, years later, they say with certainty that God has certainly helped them. That life-changing Christmas was the beginning of a journey which they never wanted, but which has never ceased to amaze them.

Within minutes, the doorbell and telephone were ringing. In the three hours before midnight, over forty people came to share their grief. Some stayed just a few silent minutes; some prayed with them and tried to encourage them; others fell apart emotionally and the Moseys had to help them! 'This support continued for several weeks,' recalls John, 'making us glad that we were part of such a very real church family. For weeks, each morning after breakfast, we would open ten to twenty envelopes which the bewildered postman had delivered. The messages that helped us most seemed to be the ones that made us cry.'

It was not until the evening following the disaster that they realised that they were going to be a focus for media attention. A TV news team arrived at the Mosey home and asked if they could interview them. One of the questions they were asked was, 'Has this destroyed your faith?' 'Well,' John replied, 'this is where we prove whether what we have preached and said we believed for most of our lives is real, or whether it is just a game.' John and Lisa now say that during the years since Helga's death, they have found the grace and love of God, and the strength that He gives, to be *more* real than they had ever previously experienced.

It wasn't until five days after the disaster that John was able to begin properly formulating his strategy for surviving this unwelcome blow to their family. At five o'clock in the morning, he sat at Helga's desk in her room at the top of their house. Nothing could alter the dreadful facts. The cry for revenge towards the terrorists was already being heard from some of the relatives of victims. John certainly agreed that the guilty parties should be brought to justice to deter others of similar mind, but he felt he could not seek personal revenge, even against those who had so cruelly murdered his nineteen-year-old daughter. He cried to God, 'Lord, I can't be like that.' John saw that if he sought revenge against his enemies, he reduced himself to their level and gave the devil 100% interest on his investment in evil men's lives. 'No,' he decided, 'our anger must be directed not against the small fry who plant bombs, but against the arch-terrorist, the force behind all the world's evils, Satan himself.' His mind went to the apostle Paul's letter to the Romans in the Bible: 'Do not be overcome by evil, but overcome evil with good.'[1]

In the weeks following Christmas, friends set up the Helga Mosey Memorial Trust for the care and education of needy children in the third world. As a result, a beautiful children's home in the Philippines has been built for abandoned and abused children. When John and Lisa visit there and see those healthy and loved kids, knowing that many of them would be dead today if Helga was alive, they feel that they have given something back.

John, a church minister, had prepared his Christmas Day sermon some days before Helga's death. As he stood to deliver it on Christmas morning, it dawned on him how apt it was. It was entitled 'The Empty Chair in Heaven'. He had decided to preach from the Bible phrase 'when the set time had fully come, God sent his Son'.[2] With tears in his eyes, he spoke about how God the Father gave up, in a sense, His immediate relationship with His son for thirty-three years. The temporary parting with their daughter and the empty chair in their home gave John some sense of relating, in human terms, to God's situation.

On Christmas Day 1988, the Moseys followed their usual routine but with little appetite and heavy hearts. They missed Helga's laugh, her help in the kitchen, her music. Their presents to her had been in her suitcase. She had left gifts at home for each of them. Marcus handed round the beautifully wrapped packages. 'To dad, with love from Helga and Marcus': a pair of gloves, almost too precious to wear. They sat quietly, desperately holding the last tangible expressions of her love for them.

They will never forget that Christmas. They remember the shock and the numbness as they did their best to cope. They recall the ache in their hearts and the physical pain of their loss. But they also remember the love and thoughtfulness of friends, neighbours and even complete strangers, and the warm support of their great Christian family. They think too of the overwhelming assurance that, although they did not understand why God had allowed this to happen, and they certainly didn't like it, somehow He knew all about it and they could trust Him and His purposes.

Less than a year later, someone said to Lisa, 'Haven't you got over it yet?' John later explained, 'The loss of someone who you love very much isn't like an illness you get over. It is more like an amputation which you learn to live with. We will feel the loss for the rest of our lives but, with God's help, we might just become better people for it.'

CHAPTER 5

THE WORLD IS RESCUED

It is natural to wonder why God doesn't stop trouble in the world. If we are moved by the suffering of others, surely God must be too. Essentially, to begin to find an answer, we need to look at Jesus Christ's death and subsequent resurrection. Christians believe this is central to all understanding of what God is doing in the world, and His intervention – or otherwise – in its problems.

The Bible teaches that Jesus is Lord of all. He came from God the Father to planet earth, living a pure life without sin or shame. Yet the people He loved so much plotted to execute Him. Many ask, *'Why did God allow such callous cruelty? Why didn't God do something when Jesus was being crucified? Why did God the Father desert His own Son at what appeared to be such a terrible time? Why did He not do something to intervene?'*

GOD ON EARTH

The Bible repeatedly says that there is only one God. He is eternal, all-powerful, all-knowing, never changing, totally just and loving, and He is everywhere. There is relationship in the Godhead, so that the one God is in three persons: Father, Son and Holy Spirit. While there is one-ness in the Trinity, there is distinctness. God, the Son, took on Himself a human body and came into the world that He had created. He was coming to rescue us from the plight of separation from Him that we had brought on ourselves.

Among the many names of Jesus is 'Immanuel', which means, 'God with us'. The God of the universe was big enough to become small; strong enough to become weak. God is not only distant but immanent, close to us, identifying Himself and involving Himself with the affairs of earth. In fact, He is *in* the world: 'In the beginning was the Word, and the Word was with God, and the Word was God … the Word became flesh and dwelt among us'[1] reads the opening of the Gospel of John, one of the Bible's biographies of Jesus. It was God's plan that, in the fullness of time, He would step into the arena of human history to reach out to and rescue men and women.[2] The Creator became like us, His creation, as He clothed Himself in a human body. God did not turn away from the suffering and sin of the world, nor wash His hands of it. Instead, He came to this earth, destined to suffer and die. Jesus, the Son of God, came alongside suffering humanity. As His mother, Mary, was a virgin, and not married at the time she gave birth, He was probably branded as 'illegitimate'. The story of the birth of Christ is well known, but the reality was not as cosy as nativity plays make out. With no place to stay, Mary had to rest her newborn baby in an animal feeding trough. When Jesus was a child, Mary and Joseph had to flee with Him as refugees to Egypt, because King Herod ordered the killing of all baby boys in Bethlehem.

Jesus knew what it was to be rejected, misunderstood, reviled, scorned and hated. He deliberately chose among His twelve disciples one who was a traitor, and who eventually sold Jesus for the price of a slave: thirty pieces of silver. Political and religious leaders, who should have known better, dogged Jesus' footsteps, trying to trap and undermine Him. Ultimately it was they who had Jesus crucified. Yet it was for this that He was born. As novelist Dorothy Sayers put it, '[God] had the honesty and the courage to take His own medicine.'[3]

The bitterness and aggression that Jesus endured was despite the fact that He went around doing good. He spread an atmosphere of love and peace as He taught the world's highest moral standard. All that He taught was simply a standard set by the way He had lived. He cured the sick, raised the dead, fed the hungry crowds and transformed for the good those who trusted Him. He went alongside the underdogs of society, cared for those who were rejected and despised, lifted up the downtrodden and forgave sins.

PHYSICAL AND EMOTIONAL SUFFERING

Eventually, though, Jesus was betrayed and arrested. He

endured a mockery of a trial, where even His judge, Pontius Pilate, asked the baying mob, 'Why, what evil has He done?'[4] Pilate's wife sent a message to her husband saying, 'Don't have anything to do with that innocent man ...'[5] The crowds howled out for His death: 'Let Him be crucified!'[6] and 'His blood be on us and on our children.'[7] After symbolically washing his hands of the death of Jesus, Pilate 'delivered Him to be crucified.'[8]

They stripped Jesus and mocked Him. He was beaten on His bare back, making it appear like a ploughed-up field. The Roman soldiers twisted a crown of thorns and put it on His sensitive brow. They put a reed in His hand, bowed the knee and gave mock praise to Jesus. They spat in His face, and struck Him with the reed.

They then dressed Him in ordinary clothes, and made Him carry His cross. He collapsed under the weight of it. No-one whom Jesus had helped or healed came to His assistance. Eventually, Simon of Cyrene was compelled to carry the cross for Jesus. When they arrived at a place called 'Golgotha', meaning 'The place of the Skull', the soldiers crucified Jesus along with two criminals. On the cross, Jesus refused the wine offered to Him. Jesus refused to swallow the drugged drink normally provided as an act of compassion to those about to be crucified; He chose to be aware of His suffering. He know that His supreme sacrifice, to be valid, must be conscious.

Dramatic events occurred at the time of crucifixion, but what was happening to Jesus was horrific. Jesus suffered physically in the way tens of thousands did who were crucified by the Romans. A description of the slow and intensely painful death of those subjected to this form of execution should be read by those in doubt as to whether Jesus really did suffer.*

---

*The Bible records Jesus' crucifixion with simple words: 'And ... they crucified Him' (Mark 15:24). However, Dr Truman Davis, in *The Expositor's Bible Commentary*, describes crucifixion in more graphic detail:

The cross is placed on the ground and the exhausted man is quickly thrown backwards with his shoulders against the wood. The legionnaire feels for the depression at the front of the wrist. He drives a heavy, square, wrought-iron nail through the wrist and deep into the wood. Quickly he moves to the other side and repeats the action, being careful not to pull the arms too tightly, but to allow some flex and movement. The cross is then lifted into place.

The left foot is pressed backward against the right foot, and with both feet extended, toes down, a nail is driven through the arch of each, leaving the knees flexed. The victim is now crucified. As he slowly sags down with more weight on the nails in the wrists, excruciating, fiery pain shoots along the fingers and up the arms to explode in the brain – the nails in the wrist are putting pressure on the median nerves. As he pushes himself upward to avoid stretching torment, he places the full weight on the nail through his feet.

Again he feels the searing agony of the nail tearing through the nerves between the bones of the feet. As the arms fatigue, cramps sweep through the muscles, knotting them in deep, relentless, throbbing pain. With these cramps comes the inability to push himself upward to breathe. Air can be drawn into the lungs but not exhaled. He fights to raise himself in order to get even one small breath. Finally, carbon dioxide builds up in the lungs and in the blood stream, and the cramps partially subside. Spasmodically he is able to push himself upward to exhale and bring in life-giving oxygen.

Hours of this limitless pain, cycles of twisting, joint-rending cramps, intermittent partial asphyxiation, searing pain as tissue is torn from his lacerated back as he moves up and down against the rough timber. Then another agony begins: a deep, crushing pain deep in the chest as the pericardium slowly fills with serum and begins to compress the heart.

It is now almost over – the loss of tissue fluids reached a critical level – the compressed heart is struggling to pump heavy, thick, sluggish blood into the tissues – the tortured lungs are making a frantic effort to gasp in small gulps of air.

He can feel the chill of death creeping through his tissues ... Finally he can allow his body to die.

As well as suffering physically, Jesus suffered emotionally. His disciples, who had given up everything to follow Him, now deserted Him and fled. One betrayed Jesus, another repeatedly denied Him, and the others cowered in fear as to what might happen to them. Cursing criminals were crucified on either side of Him, and the howling mob of political and religious leaders, along with ordinary citizens, hurled verbal abuse at the crucified Christ. However, the worst aspect of the cross of Christ is that He suffered spiritually.

SPIRITUAL SUFFERING

Throughout His teaching, Jesus repeatedly spoke of His death by crucifixion.[9] These were not the words of a gloomy pessimist. Jesus had come to die, the ultimate purpose of His suffering being to take on Himself the sin of the world. We read that Christ '… gave Himself for our sins, that He might deliver us from this present evil age, according to the will of our God and Father'.[10] The greatest work that Jesus would do was to die.

God, who is absolutely just, satisfied His own justice against all the wrong doing of the world as Jesus died on the cross. Jesus took on Himself the sin of the world and God's rightful anger against it. Jesus died as the substitute sacrifice as He paid the penalty for our wrong, so that we might be forgiven and be declared free by God. At the cross, God's love for us and justice against sin met together.

God, who hates all wrongdoing, took the sin of the world and laid it on Jesus. He paid the cost of our sin so that the barrier of sin, which separates us from God, might be removed. Because sin can be forgiven, we can be reconciled to God. Jesus' death was the world's greatest act of love, 'For the grace of God that brings salvation has appeared to all men … our great God and Saviour, Jesus Christ … gave Himself for us, that He might redeem us from every lawless deed and purify for Himself His own special people, zealous for good works.'[11] Jesus was made guilty, so that we who are actually guilty might be forgiven. He carried the can for our sin, so that all ours might be removed. Our unrighteousness was laid on Jesus the sinless One, so that we could be declared sinless in the sight of God.

When the late Pope John Paul II saw a video version of Mel Gibson's film *The Passion of Christ*, it was reported that he said, 'It is as it was.'[12] However, although the film may have successfully portrayed Christ's physical sufferings, no-one can ever depict Jesus' death as it was. The significance of the cross of Jesus is not only His physical or emotional sufferings, but His act of carrying the weight of the world's sin on Himself. God transformed what appeared a sad and tragic end to a good life into what was to be the greatest benefit for the world. Jesus is the Saviour who Himself has suffered and gone through death. God devised a means whereby we who should be banished can be brought near to Him through the achievement of the sacrifice of His Son.

As Jesus entered the hours of suffering on the cross, He prayed, 'Father, forgive them, for they do not know what they are doing.'[13] When Jesus had paid for our sin, and was about to give up His life, He prayed in a loud voice, 'Father, into Your hands I commit My spirit.'[14] The Bible records that after crying this, Jesus breathed His last breath. However, as Christ was suffering, '[He] cried out with a loud voice, *"Eloi, Eloi, lama sabachthani"* (which means, "My God, my God, why have You forsaken Me?").'[15] As Christ was bearing the sin of the world, He could only speak to God as God, and not as His Father. God turned away from His Son because Jesus was made 'to be sin for us'.[16] He was forsaken by God the Father, so that we might be forgiven and never forsaken by God. He took our separation from God on Himself, so that we could know and experience God's presence through all life's journey. Mysteriously and wonderfully, such was the horrendous happening of Jesus dying for us that a separation of the Father and Son occurred. Out of love for us, and a desire that we be freed from the mess we're in, Jesus took on Himself all that should be ours – including the gulf between us and God. He became our substitute.

FORGIVENESS FOR ALL

Whatever our sins, there is forgiveness to all who genuinely and sincerely turn from them to God, who is infinitely merciful. Guilt creates its own suffering. Albert Speer was a confidante of Hitler and whose technological genius was credited with keeping Nazi factories humming throughout World War II. He was the only one of the twenty-four criminals tried in Nuremberg to admit his guilt. Speer spent twenty years in Spandau prison. He later said, 'I served a sentence of twenty years, and I could say, "I'm a free man, my conscience has been cleared by serving the whole time as punishment." But I can't do that. I still carry the burden of what happened to millions of people during Hitler's lifetime, and I can't get rid of it.'[17] His writings are filled with contrition and warnings to others to avoid his moral sin. He desperately wanted expiation. Because of what Jesus accomplished on the cross, there is the offer of forgiveness to those who will repent and believe. As the Bible expresses it, 'the blood of Jesus Christ [God's] Son cleanses us from all sin ... If we confess our sins, He is faithful and just to forgive us ours sins and to cleanse us from all unrighteousness.'[18]

POWER OVER DEATH

God's ability to transform the worst situation is demonstrated in Jesus' death and resurrection. After His death, He was taken by friends and buried in a previously unused tomb. There His body, wrapped in cloths and with His head wrapped separately, lay, cold, still, dead. The tomb was sealed, and guarded by Roman soldiers. For three days and nights, He lay in the cave. Then, on the first 'Easter morning', the light of the rising sun revealed that the stone had rolled away and the body of Jesus had gone, even though strips of linen were lying there, as well as the separate burial cloth that had been around Jesus' head.[19] Jesus had risen from the dead. This was no 'conjuring trick with bones'.[20] There is a huge amount of evidence from Christian, Jewish and Roman writers of the day testifying to the supernatural happenings around the death and resurrection of Jesus.[21] It is an aspect of the life and work of Jesus Christ that marks Him out as being utterly unique. It demonstrates God's power to bring life out of death, and victory out of apparent 'defeat'.

In a broadcast through the world's media on 23 December 2003, Samantha Roberts, the widow of the first soldier killed in the Iraq War, was interviewed. She told how she had met President George W. Bush when he had made a state visit to the UK a month earlier. She recalled standing before 'the most powerful man on the earth, but he couldn't bring back my husband.' Only Jesus is 'the way, the truth and the life.'[22] He could not allow himself to be taken hostage, even by death. Those who put their faith and trust in Christ find that, by His Holy Spirit, He gives life – that takes a person through death and into eternity with Him.

CASE STUDY 3

NAME: Diane

SITUATION: Young person struggling with
chronic pain

Diane was brought up on a farm in the country, before moving to Leeds to study design. 'I wanted to make it big in the design world, and it was always my goal to be the very best at what I did, even in a very competitive world.' Although her family were Christians, Diane had been far from God for many years. It was following a humanitarian trip to Ukraine, and while she was working and living in Glasgow, that, as she puts it, 'I met God in a real way.' This changed her life, and from a career perspective, she felt she now wanted to serve God. An opportunity came up for her to be a designer in a Christian organisation 'where I could use the gifts and skills He had given me, and give them back to Him.' She was in her mid-twenties.

Five months into this new job, Diane started to have a terrible headache – a headache which didn't lift for three months. She kept working through this time, thinking it would be a passing problem. But then her neck and shoulder also began to give her great pain along with the headaches. It was increasingly difficult to hold down a full-time job because the pain was so intense and uncomfortable.

'What was most frustrating was that no-one could put their finger on the cause of the pain.' As a teenager, she had been through the serious, but fairly routine, operation for scoliosis. This involves attaching metal rods to straighten a curved spine. Eleven years later, she started having related problems and went through two years of investigations, treatments, injections, medications and pain clinics before she finally had an operation to relieve her shoulder pain. For three years following this, she lived with a low, manageable level of pain in her head, neck and shoulder – all above her metal rods. Unfortunately, this improvement was short-lived. Very intense pain started to develop in her lower back – below the rods – and, over the course of a year, progressed into her legs and feet.

'The fear of another episode of pain-filled days, endless waiting lists, different medications and no real answers to explain the pain set in.' She had been investigating joining a mission organisation and had hopes for this new opportunity, but was devastated that she could no longer pursue this: 'It was the worst thing. I had to accept all over again the reality of the term "chronic pain". The simplest task, such as washing the dishes, was exhausting because the pain was so wearing. Often I would feel that my body was covered in pain from head to foot – quite literally: bad headaches; neck and shoulder pain; pins and needles in my arms; my lower back burning with pain; pain down my legs; and painful feet.'

Looking back on that year, she says, 'It was a year of disappointments, due to a body which constantly let me down. I have a heart to serve God, yet I haven't had the answer I want to my pleading prayer which says, 'Heal me so I can serve You.' Nothing has made sense to me during this time, and I still wonder at what God is doing in my life.' She read God's promise in the Bible that '… in all things God works for the good of those who love [Him] …'[1] and asked, 'If that's right, that everything is for God's glory, where is the glory He sees in my pain?'

At a particularly low time, when these questions were constantly invading her head, when she couldn't see God in her pain or in her day, she decided, 'to pull myself together and seek Him. If I couldn't see Him, I would have to try and find Him. He promised, "You will seek Me and find Me, when you search for Me with all your heart"[2] – so I went looking.'

At this dramatic turning point, when all seemed quite desperate, Diane sought God and found Him in a fresh and real way: 'I saw Him most beautifully in creation. I read verses in the Bible where Jesus says, "I am the Alpha and Omega, the Beginning and the End"[3] in a new light. I began to look forward to the better things to come, that He has promised; to a time when there will be no pain, when God will wipe every tear.[4]

And this time, when Diane thought that no doctor could understand her pain and help her, God reminded her of Jesus' promise: 'Come to Me, all you who labour and are heavy laden, and I will give you rest. Take My yoke upon you and learn from Me, for I am gentle and lowly in heart and you will find rest for your souls. For My yoke is easy and My burden is light.'[5] As she waited on Him, He cleared the way for the right doctors to come to light and bring new hope. She still doesn't know the future outcome, but is awaiting an operation which may or may not work, and at least is offering a glimmer of hope. 'God has said, "I go before you," and I trust that. He knows the way I take.'

This whole experience has been a huge disappointment to Diane. Big questions remain unanswered: 'Why, when every area of my life is for God – my friendships, my business, my church life – does He not take away my pain? Why, when He has the power to remove it, does He allow so much pain to run riot in my body?' She continues, 'Sometimes we have to live with unanswered questions, but I can't help feeling that I could do so much more without this hindrance in my life. But Jesus suffered, and in all ways is making us more like Him, so perhaps this suffering is an honour? Maybe it gives me a taster – and only a taster – of what He went through for me?'

Over the years, Diane has found comfort from Job in the Bible. He suffered yet he still praised God. 'He suffered and, over time, he got tired and worn down. I know this worn-out feeling. He questioned God, and God replied asking Job who he is to question Almighty God. When I think of this, I am humbled because I realise how mighty God is. I am glad for my suffering at times because it makes me rely more fully on God, who is the Maker of all things.'

Without an eternal perspective, Diane acknowledges she would be without hope. On top of her pain-filled days and her disappointment over her career, her house was devastated by a freak flood in her home city of Carlisle. It has made her focus on the future, and see that this world is temporary and falling apart. 'We have so much better to come in eternity. Even though it is hard at times, we must hold on to the hope that we have in Christ because this world is full of disappointment. The only certainty we have is Christ, and the future He promises to those who trust in Him. I know that my future is sealed and I know that, for me, one day I will be free from a body that lets me down. I will be in heaven, with my new body, rejoicing with God – my Creator, and my Deliverer.'

CHAPTER 6

THE WORLD AS IT WILL BE

When Jesus began His three years of preaching, healing and teaching, He chose twelve men to be with Him, to teach and to train. They were to be alongside Him in all His work. The youngest of these was John, who was to outlive the others. He is the author of the Gospel of John, plus some letters found in the New Testament of the Bible and the final book of the whole Bible, the Book of Revelation. John was imprisoned for his faith in Christ on the island of Patmos in the Mediterranean Sea. On this desolate island, surrounded by the surging sea, it is as if God pulled back a curtain to give John a glimpse of eternity. The Book of Revelation, which describes this, has to be the greatest futurama of all time. Nearing the end of the vision which John describes, he saw the new heaven and the new earth:

Now I saw a new heaven and a new earth, for the first heaven and the first earth had passed away. Also

there was no more sea. Then I, John, saw the holy city,
New Jerusalem, coming down out of heaven from God,
prepared as a bride adorned for her husband. And I heard
a loud voice from heaven saying, 'Behold, the tabernacle
of God is with men, and He will dwell with them, and
they shall be His people. God Himself will be with them
and be their God. And God will wipe away every tear
from their eyes; there shall be no more death, nor sorrow,
nor crying. There shall be no more pain, for the former
things have passed away.'

Then He who sat on the throne said, 'Behold, I make all
things new.' And He said to me, 'Write, for these words
are true and faithful.'

And He said to me, 'It is done! I am the Alpha and the
Omega, the Beginning and the End. I will give of the
fountain of the water of life freely to him who thirsts.
He who overcomes shall inherit all things, and I will
be his God and he shall be My son. But the cowardly,
unbelieving, abominable, murderers, sexually immoral,
sorcerers, idolaters, and all liars shall have their part in
the lake which burns with fire and brimstone, which is
the second death.'[1]

This graphic description is of something which seems
alien to us. Nobody likes tears, but in heaven God will
wipe away all tears. We don't particularly like darkness,
but in heaven there will be no more night. We go to great

lengths to avoid pain, but in heaven there will be no more pain. We hate death, and in heaven nobody dies. We dislike any kind of sorrow, but the inhabitants of heaven do not weep. No-one likes separation, but in heaven there will be no more sea, the ultimate symbol of separation. It is a place of unclouded day, where God's reign and goodness is supreme.

This means that death can be a moment of release for some. Only God holds the keys of death, so for us to take the life of an individual to relieve their suffering is to play God and that cannot be right. Nevertheless, there are times when one looks on a situation where there has been a death and finds comfort in the thought that the deceased has gone to be with God, and is relieved of their suffering.

Hansie Cronje had for six years been the greatly loved and respected South African cricket captain. He was a genuine Christian believer. Foolishly, he became involved in match fixing and was banned from playing representative cricket for life. On 1 June 2002, he was killed in a plane crash. Surprisingly, Cronje's mother later suggested that perhaps it had been a blessing that her son had died. She said that he had suffered so much, had lost all his confidence and would have had to bear the consequences of the match-fixing scandal for the rest of his life. Cricket coach Ali Bacher said, 'That summed up the whole tragedy for me; a mother suggesting that only in death could her son be freed from his burden.'[2] Her confidence that things would be better for her son after death was clearly not based on the thought that he was good enough for heaven, but on the fact that he was trusting Christ to forgive all that would condemn him.

ETERNAL TROUBLE

Most of us give little time or thought to considering even the possibility of an afterlife. Yet it is something we should not ignore. The passage above, from the Book of Revelation, also teaches that there is a place of eternal trouble. The Bible warns of hell, a punishment after life on earth. God is absolutely just and righteous. Rejection of Him and His ways has a penalty. Jesus, who loved so much, warned that God, who is just by nature, must punish sin. There is ultimate justice. So we read that those who are unbelieving in mind and actions – those who have rejected God's remedy for forgiveness and reconciliation with Himself – will pay their own penalty for their own sin. They have refused the gift of eternal life through Jesus Christ the Lord, and therefore receive the consequences of their sin.[3] It is hard to imagine a more serious theme.

Gwyn Williams was for some time a pastor of a church in Port Talbot in Wales. He was once given a tour of their famous steel works. He was walking high up on a gantry when the guide revealed how a man had fallen from there into the furnace's 3000 degrees of white heat below. Gwyn Williams tried to imagine the horror of the man as he fell and thought that to be drawn into the holiness of God without the protection of Christ must be something similar.

Jesus Himself, out of love for us, warned of the consequences of stubbornly refusing Him; not for His own selfish or egotistical purposes, but because He longed for people to enjoy God and His creation in the way He intended it. His heart's desire was towards people, even though they may be extremely wayward. After exposing and berating the hypocrisy of the religious leaders of His day in Jerusalem, Jesus cried, 'Jerusalem, Jerusalem, you who kill the prophets and stone those sent to you, how often I have longed to gather your children together, as a hen gathers her chicks under her wings, but you were not willing.'[4]

If God is perfectly just, and that is how He has revealed Himself, then we would expect God to act fairly and finally towards those who reject Him, choosing to live contrary to the ways and laws that He has shown. There is something in human minds also which demands that there be more than just the tame punishments of society's courts towards grossly wicked people. It does not seem right that Hitler could bring his existence to an end simply by pulling a trigger. He, along with millions of others, will be judged by God; their eternal destiny will depend on what they have done with God and the gift of salvation, which was offered to them.

Every nation, leader and individual will appear before God, who will be their judge. I am often asked if all religions lead to God. The answer is that every religion, even atheism, leads to God, for everyone will meet Him. Either they will appear before God as their Judge or as

WHERE IS GOD IN A MESSED-UP WORLD

their welcoming Father. Jesus said, 'I am the way, the truth, and the life. No one comes to the Father except through Me.'⁵ After death, every individual will meet God on the throne of judgement or on the throne of grace and mercy.

Towards the end of the Bible, there is a graphic vision of God's court room:

> *Then I saw a great white throne and Him who was seated on it. The earth and the heavens fled from His presence, and there was no place for them. And I saw the dead, great and small, standing before the throne, and books were opened. Another book was opened, which is the book of life. The dead were judged according to what they had done as recorded in the books. The sea gave up the dead that were in it, and death and Hades gave up the dead that were in them, and each person was judged according to what they had done. Then death and Hades were thrown into the lake of fire. The lake of fire is the second death. Anyone whose name was not found written in the book of life was thrown into the lake of fire.*⁶

Harold S. Kushner, the North American Jewish Rabbi, caused a stir with his book entitled *When Bad Things Happen to Good People.*⁷ However, bad things can happen to bad people too. Life is not to be merely seen from a current perspective but from God's vantage point, which is an eternal view of events. Yet there is a brighter side to eternity that can transform the heart and mind of any who will turn from all that is wrong in their lives, and trust Jesus Christ as their Lord, Saviour and Friend. For the Christian, there is no need to fear death. The 'sting' of death is our sin, but Christ has taken that sting Himself, and therefore there is nothing of which to be afraid.

FUTURE PERSPECTIVE

In AD 155, the city of Smyrna was the scene of religious amusement. Statius Quadratus, the Roman proconsul, was the guest of honour. As part of the entertainment, eleven Christians were brought in from Philadelphia to be thrown to the lions. The excitement of the people reached its peak. 'Polycarp! Polycarp!' they yelled. They searched for the greatly loved Christian leader. When he was found, he was brought to the stadium. The proconsul tried in vain to persuade Polycarp to deny the lordship of Jesus Christ, but only received the reply: 'Eighty-six years I have served Him, and He never did me wrong. How can I blaspheme my King who has saved me?' He was tied to a stake, flaming wood was placed on his aged body, and there he was martyred. His remains were buried on Mount Pagus.[8]

Centuries later, John Bradford, prebendary of St Paul's, was imprisoned in the Tower of London because of his Protestant faith in Christ. On 1 July 1555, he was martyred. He was chained to the stake at Smithfield with a young man, John Leaf. Before the fire was lit, he begged forgiveness of any he had wronged, and offered forgiveness to those who had wronged him. He then turned to Leaf and said, 'Be of good comfort brother; for we shall have a merry supper with the Lord this night!' Christians have the certainty of heaven for heaven is not a reward for doing good, but a gift purchased by Jesus and offered to all.

Having an eternal, future perspective on life is the attempt to see the world as God sees it. The effect of that is startling. For example, Psalm 73, written by Asaph, begins with an affirmation that God is good to His people, but then articulates the serious questions that had caused doubts in his mind. Asaph could not be ostrich-like and bury his head in the sand; there were things that perplexed him. It seemed to him that wicked people prospered, while those who tried to follow the laws of God did so in vain because they suffered. He honestly and frankly tells God his concerns. As one reads, it seems as though his doubts will lead to cynicism. But then there is a change. The questioning continues until a moment in the psalm that is pivotal. Asaph begins to look at the situation from an eternal point of view. He ponders not only the life of people on earth but their eternity, and the blessing that God gives to those who are trusting in Him. He realises that the snapshots of society with which he was being confronted are not the full story. In contrast to God, he is not everywhere, at all times. Not all Asaph's questions are answered, but enjoying the fact that God was close to him enables Asaph to rest in renewed confidence that God knew what He is doing. Asaph revels in the fact that God is a precious friend to him and is more significant than anything else. He says, with renewed confidence, 'Whom have I in heaven but You? And there is none upon earth that I desire besides You.'[9] He ends his psalm with the words: 'But it is good for me to draw near to God; I have put my trust in the Lord God, that I may declare all Your works.'[10] And there he rests.

CASE STUDY 4

NAME: Laura

SITUATION: Thirty-something battling with terminal cancer

Laura was successful in many ways; a bright girl, she studied at Oxford University and went on to have a high-flying career in sales and marketing. She had become a Christian before going to university, and seemed sorted in her beliefs. Her faith was based on believing what the Bible says about human nature to be true, and how this applied directly to her own life. 'As I came to understand a little more of God's character, the worst thing was realising quite how that applied to me … the Bible was teaching me the truth about what I was like, and [that] I couldn't change my heart.' She came to realise that though she couldn't change her heart, God could. Deciding to follow and trust in Jesus Christ was tested intellectually during her time at Oxford: 'University was such a challenge to my faith as students do talk about ideas and are really willing to challenge your faith … Time and again I found myself trying to show my friends that there was historical evidence for Christ's existence and for Him being who

He said He was – God Himself, who was made man.'

This confidence was to be tested in a poignant way a few years later when she was struck by a brain haemorrhage during a meeting at work. She found herself in hospital awaiting a major operation, with a possibility of facing brain damage, or death. 'As I lay there in the hospital, I knew God had me in His hands and, no matter what happened in the operation – whether I woke up or not, I was safe. I knew He had promised me life after death, and that I would go on somewhere better. That feeling of incredible security and peace was amazing.'

'I remember at the time I was calling people and saying goodbye to them. My poor friends had just heard about what had happened, and on the phone I was saying, "I'm going to be okay, I'm in God's hands whatever happens." I think I upset a few friends!'

Laura came round from the operation and all was well. She felt God had given her an amazing gift of life. So she wanted to use it by spending most of her time helping Christian students to grow in their faith and understanding of God and the Bible, and to tell others about Jesus Christ.

Six years later, though, she was again confronted with major health issues. She was diagnosed with skin cancer. At first, the doctors couldn't give an accurate prognosis, but as time progressed, the cancer spread. It was later confirmed that Laura had tumours in both her lungs. Almost two years after first discovering the skin cancer, she said, 'Although I look perfectly healthy, I am dying. It is just taking a lot longer for me to die than we originally thought, which I'm glad about. Obviously I had to think very hard about what I believed and whether it was true.'

It is quite rare to die of cancer in your thirties. Laura reflected, 'God helped me in a number of ways to cope with dying at a relatively young age. There are promises in the Bible about death. Jesus Christ said that He came to die. Once He was talking to some women who had just lost their brother, Lazarus, who had been dead and buried in a tomb for four days. He was also a good friend of Jesus. The comfort Jesus gives these women is a bit strange. He said, 'I am the resurrection and the life. He who believes in Me, though he may die, he shall live. And whoever lives and believes in Me shall never die. Do you believe this?'[1] This is a man claiming that He has the whole key to life and death wrapped up in His very self. Then, to prove it, He spoke just one word and His friend Lazarus came out of the tomb after being dead for four days.

'This was recorded by eyewitnesses. Then Jesus went on to die Himself and rise from the dead. For me this is the real guarantee that there is life after death. Jesus rose from the dead, and therefore He has been through death ahead of me. I do not have to fear death. God has promised that for those who love

Him, there is a life to come that Christ knows about and He is there. That life has none of the tears and the hurt and the things that we do to one another that ruin this world; it's a perfect world. That for me is an incredible comfort. I know that at the end of life, there is something better to come, which has really kept me going. God has given me promises for my death.'

Laura also found that God had given her promises for life. The experience of the brain haemorrhage had changed her attitude: 'I knew my feeling of peace and security was supernatural. I haven't ever been worried about death since that, and I think that has been quite a help for this and for coping with cancer.'

God's promise to stay with His people was also a source of hope for Laura. Many years ago, God said, 'And the Lord, He is the One who goes before you. He will be with you, He will not leave you nor forsake you; do not fear nor be dismayed.'[2] In Laura's own words, '… that's certainly true in my life. Every morning, I wake up and I don't know if another symptom will show itself, or if it will be the day I go to hospital and hear more bad news. The hardest thing about all this has been my having to tell my family and friends more and more bad news. So every day, I get up but I can't step outside of my body, and go on a holiday, and forget about the fact that I am ill. I have to live with it. I have just been so amazed at how God has stepped in every time I've asked for help and said I can't cope with this. As I've cried out to Him and said, 'Today is going to be a real struggle, God,' He has stepped in and has kept me so calm, and so at peace, and so joyful.'

'I can truly say that I haven't had a day of despair since this cancer was diagnosed and further diagnosis revealed I'm dying. I've had hard times and shocking news. I've had really difficult phone conversations and times with family and friends. But God has been there in all of it and kept me calm and at peace. And I've never really asked the question, 'Why?' It's just been incredible to experience the love of a God who can keep us calm and happy in what have been quite difficult circumstances. He has given me hope for the future in my death, but He has also provided incredible support in my life. Again, I have to say that can only be supernatural, because I'm certainly not a calm person normally. It has actually been amazing to experience it.'

To crowds of students at Cambridge University, about ten months before she died, Laura said, 'When you face death, I want you to know there is something good to go on to. You can die with confidence in the arms of a loving Father, knowing you are safe and that you are His child. It has been great living out my life as a child of God. It has been wonderful – the best part of my life! I want you to know, like I do, that whatever happens to you tomorrow, you are secure. You can know that God loves you; that nothing can happen that He can't protect you from and keep you safe throughout.'

SECTION THREE

CHAPTER 7

CHANGE

Leo Tolstoy was an orphaned son of a Russian nobleman. He left his university studies without a degree, fought in the Crimean War, wrote several acclaimed short novels, and experimented with progressive education for children – all before he married the eighteen-year-old Sofia Andreyevna Behrs in 1862. The couple raised nineteen children. He is particularly remembered for his two great novels, *War and Peace* and *Anna Karenina*. In an autobiographical note he wrote:

> *Five years ago I came to believe in Christ's teaching, and my life suddenly changed; I ceased to desire what I had previously desired, and began to desire what I formerly did not want. What had previously seemed to me good seemed evil, and what seemed evil seemed good. It happened to me as it happens to a man who goes out on some business and on the way suddenly decides that the*

business is unnecessary and returns home. All that was on his right is now on his left, and all that was on his left is now on his right; his former wish to get as far as possible from home has changed into a wish to be as near as possible to it. The direction of my life and my desires became different, and good and evil changed places ...

I, like the thief on the cross, knew that I was unhappy and suffering. I, like the thief on the cross, was nailed by some force to a life of suffering and evil. And as, after the meaningless sufferings and evils of life, the thief awaited the terrible darkness of death, so did I await the same thing ...

But suddenly I heard the words of Christ and understood them, and life and death ceased to seem evil, and instead of despair I experienced happiness and the joy of life undisturbed by death.[1]

Many Christians, in vastly different cultures, ages and situations, have experienced a similar distinct change of heart and mind as they surrendered their life and future to Jesus Christ. Their life, from that moment, with its highs and lows, would never be the same.

Being a Christian essentially means being a follower of Jesus Christ. This not only involves trusting in Him as Lord and Saviour, but following His example and attitude to this broken world. In the Bible we read, '... if anyone is in Christ, he is a new creation; old things have passed away … all things have become new.'² The Christian experiences not only forgiveness from sin but a new perspective on life. They see beyond the immediate, and can look forward to a new world – a new creation encompassing heaven and earth. The Bible speaks of a time yet to come when people will be reconciled to God and to one another through Jesus Christ. A taste of this should be evident in the way that Christians today relate to each other and the world around them.

CULTIVATING RELATIONSHIP

There are those who cynically say that Christianity is merely a psychological prop. Christianity is more than a crutch to lean on. Rather, it is a vibrant relationship with God Himself, and one that prepares and takes a person through each season of life. God may be called upon at any moment, but those who know Him in the stable times of life are the ones who are ready for the storms of life.

Todd Beamer, who was on United Airlines Flight 93 bound for San Francisco on 11 September 2001, had such a relationship with God. When the plane was hijacked, he is the one who spoke those unforgettable words, 'Let's roll!' as they set about taking on the hijackers. Shortly afterwards, the plane crashed in a remote area of Pennsylvania. In his wife's account of losing her husband in a terrorist attack, she shares how she found on their computer her husband's description of his relationship with God:

I have had stops and starts in building my relationship with God … I screw up, I let Him down, and I do not always spend time with God the way I should. This is because I am trying to force the relationship and steer it in the direction I want it to go. That doesn't work, and only leads to frustration.

However, each time I come to God to ask for forgiveness, He is there for me. Each time I ask God for help, He is there for me. Each time I cry out in frustration and pain, He is there for me.

While my relationship with God is far from perfect … God has been there for me time and again, and has expressed His love and grace for me. Although at times I have taken God for granted … my experience has been that God is patient and waiting for us to come to Him. Once we come to Him and give more of our lives to Him, He will give more of Himself to us.[3]

Not every Christian faces such dramatic circumstances, but we each face the reality of death. Having a relationship with God, through Jesus Christ, means that death can be faced with confidence. Death for the Christian is not the end, but the beginning of an eternity with the God they know and trust.

A friend of mine, Peter Frost, was a committed Christian. He worked in business and was married to Kathy, with whom he had a young son, Jonah. There was always something a little mischievous about this constantly cheerful man. When he was in his early thirties, however, he was diagnosed with leukaemia. The medical upheavals he would face were a most unenviable period in his life, but during this painful time he developed a most intimate knowledge of God. A few months before he died, he wrote a short note to me:

Dear Roger,

Just a quick note to say that I was admitted for a bone marrow transplant. I am at the Heath Hospital in Cardiff and expect to be here for a month or so (in isolation). It is a miracle that we have come this far – especially since my total relapse last November. At that stage this 'window of opportunity' was not open to us, but graciously God has brought us to this place.

We don't know what the short- or medium-term outcome will hold for us, but we do hope – not in an outcome, but in a Person. I was reading in Hebrews 6:16-20 – Jesus promises this to us 'in His own name and He cannot lie'. 'We have this hope as an anchor for the soul, firm and secure …' I was reading an old Welsh hymn the other day and the last two lines of each verse read: 'too wise to make mistakes; too good to be unkind' …

Peter

CHANGING PERSPECTIVE

Some of the most wonderful words of comfort found in the Bible are right at the end, in the second to last chapter of the Book of Revelation. The ageing disciple, John, is describing the close of his vision, when he saw the new heavens and the new earth. He records the words of God Himself, as heard in the vision about the dwelling place of God, that He will dwell with His people and God Himself 'will be with them and be their God. He will wipe every tear from their eyes. There will be no more death or mourning or crying or pain, for the old order of things has passed away.'[4]

Those who are trusting in Christ as their only means of reconciliation with God are indeed reconciled to Him. God will live with them, and they will be free from pain, suffering, disaster, disappointment, fear, brutality, grief, death, inequality, poverty and injustice. It is hard to imagine something so perfect and unspoilt, but it is a promise from the mouth of God Himself, and is offered to anyone who accepts God's desire to rescue us from the mess of this world.

There is such freedom and relief to know that ultimately, whatever life appears to deal to a person, something better is coming. Though God's judgement is real, heaven is guaranteed to everyone who has come to know God in their lives. Lord Hailsham, twice Lord Chancellor, and therefore the highest judge in Great Britain, expressed this well when he said, 'When I die and stand before God in judgement, I will plead guilty and cast myself upon the mercy of the court.' The assurance of heaven – freed from God's judgement – is the *incentive* that gives hope, the *comfort* that gives strength, and the *confidence* that gives calm.

CHAPTER 8

COMFORT

Three months before he died, I received a letter from Professor David Short, the retired Professor of Medicine at Aberdeen University, who had been the Queen's physician in Scotland. After some pleasantries, he wrote:

A few days before setting out on our winter holiday in Spain, my wife and I got a health shock. We haven't time to tell all our friends the news but we would like you to hear it direct from us. A routine blood test showed that I have acute myeloid leukaemia. The consultant haematologist discussed treatment and felt that current radical therapy is more trouble than it is worth. Whatever is done, the prognosis is measured in weeks or months. The holiday in Spain was perfect and at present I remain as well as ever.

He then quoted first the Bible and then the Victorian

preacher and author C.H. Spurgeon, who saw death like crossing a river:

Isaiah 43, verses 1–2 come to me with great comfort at this time. 'Fear not, for I have redeemed you ... you are mine. When you pass through the waters, I will be with you; and when you pass through the rivers, they will not sweep over you.' And Spurgeon's comment: 'There is no bridge and no ferry-boat. We must go through the waters and feel the rush of the river. The presence of God in the flood is better than a ferry-boat. The sorrows of life may rise to an extraordinary height, but the Lord is equal to every occasion. We are precious to God. He paid an incalculable price for our salvation. We belong to Him. Since He paid so much for us, He is never going to part with us. Whatever happens, He will be with us.'

Changing the metaphor, David then closed by saying:

We would both value your prayers: that I may be enabled to run the last lap well and that Joan may have special help from God.

FACING GRIEF

Grief is the heaviness of heart caused by loss. It comes uninvited, and is not in a hurry to leave us. The Bible teaches that it is only a matter of time before it is our time to mourn. Its effects are draining, debilitating and even destructive. The loss is not necessarily of a person but may be of a job, of health or of a reputation.

Grief is both natural and right provided it doesn't become self-pitying or vengeful. The need to grieve and express profound sorrow is entrenched deep within the human psyche. The pain caused by loss can be overwhelming, numbing and relentless.

Everyone's grief is unique and individual. Some recover more quickly, others need lots of time. King David, who we read of in the Bible, lost a baby son and an adult son. He recovered quickly over the baby, but the death of Absalom was very destructive to him. In fact, the Bible has stories of those grieving over the loss of a child, a sibling, a monarch or political leader, a spouse, a friend dying before there was a chance to say goodbye, and friends where there was a farewell. Whatever the situation, we are never the same again after such losses. Like a person who has had a limb amputated, we can learn to live with the loss, but we are not going to be as once we were. Those who lost a loved one during the coronavirus pandemic in 2020 but were unable to be with them when they died felt the grief doubly deeply. Others were pained as they were not permitted to attend the funeral and pay their last respects. Grief is very painful.

And yet people have found – just as did David Short and his wife, Joan, also a doctor – that it is possible to have confidence in the crisis of death, both before and after bereavement. That certainty is given as a person faces death, and as another reflects on the loss that is causing so much hurt. The knowledge that God exists, that He is at the centre of everything – controlling all events and circumstances – and that He has defeated death – through the death and resurrection of Jesus – is wonderfully reassuring.

There is calm and rest in remembering that God is too wise to make mistakes and too good to be unkind. That doesn't mean that there is no need to grieve or sorrow. God doesn't make those who trust Him hard-nosed, insensitive autonomists. Instead, God promises to be with His people – we have become children, His sons and daughters – to give them the resources to cope with their hurts, to heal the broken-hearted.

The importance of relationships is never seen so dramatically as when one is faced with loss and bereavement. There can be regrets over words said, or unsaid; of wrong priorities; of actions and failures; or of lack of intimacy or time with the person who has gone. In moments of such grief, it is best to be honest with God, telling Him all our thoughts and regrets. The Bible encourages us to cast our cares on God knowing that He cares for us.[1] If the grief seems arbitrary, meaningless and unfair, we can give the questions and issues to God in prayer. In time, He may explain what we are going through, but in the meantime, we can at least trust Him as we go through the sorrow.

Jesus drank deeply from the cup of suffering as He faced crucifixion. Like a weightlifter concentrates intensely before actually attempting to lift the bars, so Jesus prayed before His execution in a garden called Gethsemane. That name means 'oil press'. It was a place where Jesus often went, and it seemed to illustrate His life and death as He was to be crushed. He was shortly to know what it was to experience every ounce of life being pressed out of Him. We read that while praying, His sweat was like drops of blood falling to the ground, such was the intensity of His suffering.[2] Then, after Gethsemane, came Golgotha or 'the place of the skull' – the hill where Jesus was crucified. The darkness which Jesus went through on the cross means that He can sympathise, encourage and strengthen all who feel forsaken in the mire of grief. He is able to draw alongside those who are discouraged, feeling there is little point to going on with life. That is exactly what He did for two of His followers after the events of His death and resurrection.

These two men were walking the seven-mile journey from Jerusalem to Emmaus. Utterly downcast and despondent because of the events that had led to Jesus' crucifixion in the last few days, they were now confused because of the reports that Jesus had risen from the dead. It was all too much for them. They had thought that Jesus was the One who was going to rescue Israel from the iron grip of the Roman Empire, which was oppressively occupying their nation. Instead, He had been callously crucified.

Then Jesus began to walk with them but the Bible says that they were prevented from recognising Him.[3] He appeared ignorant of all that had gone on so the two travellers quickly took their opportunity to retell the story and express their bitter disappointment. Jesus walked and listened before turning first to rebuke them for their slowness to believe and then, from the Old Testament, to explain that what had happened was what had been prophesied. They later said their hearts were 'burning within us'[4] as Jesus opened the Scriptures to them, opened their minds so that they could understand the Scriptures, and then opened their eyes to recognise Him. Once these two followers of Jesus and His disciples began to understand that what had happened to Jesus had been prophesied long before, they received great peace and happiness. Jesus said, 'Thus it is written, and thus it was necessary for the Christ to suffer and to rise from the dead the third day, and that repentance and [forgiveness] of sins should be preached in His name to all nations …'[5]

Grief is such a nasty pain, it is hard to imagine any palliative to cure the hurt. However, without appearing to be at all glib, even in such a time of trouble there is help in the person of Jesus Christ. The apostle Paul, who penned so much of our New Testament, wrote to the fledgling church in Thessalonica reminding them that 'we do not want you to be uninformed about those who sleep in death, so that you do not grieve like the rest of mankind, who have no hope.'[6] He then explained that the death and rising again of Jesus, coupled with the certainty that one day Jesus will return as Lord and ruler of all, gives cause for great comfort when one would naturally sorrow.

FINDING COMFORT

The Book of Psalms, in the middle of the Bible, is an ancient book of songs and praise to God. Reading through the 150 Psalms, there is recurring dual theme: life is tough, but God is good. Over the centuries, thousands of people have found comfort through reading and meditating on the psalms.

In Psalm 42, the author is going through dark times. He wisely speaks to his innermost being and reminds himself not to doubt in the darkness what God had shown him in brighter times:

> *Why are you cast down, O my soul?*
> *And why are you disquieted within me?*
> *Hope in God; for I shall yet praise Him ...[7]*

A couple of sentences later we read:

> *The Lord will command His lovingkindness in the daytime,*
> *and in the night His song shall be with me –*
> *a prayer to the God of my life.[8]*

The idea of 'songs in the night', or comfort in the darkest of times, has been the experience of many Christians. Paul and Silas, two early followers of Jesus Christ, were imprisoned for their faith in Philippi. They had been beaten, and put in a damp, cold prison. Yet we read that at midnight they sang praises to God.[9]

In Psalm 42 above, we also read the phrase 'the God of my life'. That phrase only occurs once in the whole Bible. The psalmist invented a new name for God, which expressed his confidence that God knew what He was doing. He trusted God, even though times were hard and the emotional structure that normally kept him in place had crumbled, leaving him totally despondent.

A favourite old, traditional hymn of Christendom is 'It Is Well with My Soul'. It was written by Horatio Spafford, a successful Chicago lawyer. In 1873, the Spafford's family doctor recommended a holiday for Mrs Spafford, so the couple made plans to travel to Europe by ship. Just before leaving, Horatio Spafford had to change his plans, and quickly arranged for his wife and four daughters to go ahead, promising to join them some days later. So she and the girls set sail without him.

On 22 November, in a tragic, freak accident, the ship was rammed and sank in less than half an hour. Mrs Spafford was rescued, but all four daughters were drowned. Later, Mrs Spafford was able to cable her husband with the stark two-word message: 'Saved alone.'

Horatio Spafford bought passage on the first ship he could find that was sailing to England. At sea, as the ship crossed the Atlantic where his daughters' bodies lay, with tears in his eyes, he penned:

When peace like a river attends my way,
When sorrows like sea billows roll;

Whatever my lot, you have taught me to say,
'It is well, it is well with my soul.'[10]

There is real comfort to be found when we trust that God is in control and we have put things right with Him. It is possible to have absolute confidence in Jesus, who said, 'I am the resurrection and the life. He who believes in Me, though he may die, he shall live. And whoever lives and believes in Me shall never die.'[11]

DEVELOPING EMPATHY

In 1944, Corrie ten Boom was taken with her family to Ravensbruck concentration camp. They had been found hiding Jews in their home in Haarlem in Holland. Most of her family died very quickly, but she and her sister Betsie survived longer. Eventually, though, Betsie was to die after being brutalised and cruelly treated. Before she died, she said to Corrie, 'If ever you get out of this place, go and tell the world that no matter how deep the pit, God is deeper still.' For forty years that is exactly what Corrie did. Her autobiography, *The Hiding Place*, honestly recalls how God met with her and blessed her in the traumas of Ravensbruck.

This by no way means that Christians can gloss over such terrors and dismiss the injustice of them, simply because somebody had a spiritual experience; nevertheless, God is able to take the worst situations here on earth and bring out of them something good and beautiful. Elie Wiesel, mentioned in chapter two, said, 'Memory is a passion no less powerful or pervasive than love.' Indeed, memories should serve to recall the past and change the future.

CHAPTER 9

FORGIVENESS

In the course of life, there will inevitably be incidents where each individual is challenged to forgive, as well as to ask for forgiveness. Petty incidents may be easier to deal with, but where the hurt cuts sharp, the need to forgive is even deeper, and it can seem an impossible task. As Oxford scholar and author C.S. Lewis put it, 'Every one says forgiveness is a lovely idea, until they have something to forgive.'[1] And yet the challenge for us is to do what God commands, and demonstrated, namely to forgive. We are used to living by rules and regulations, but Christ teaches that life is to be lived by love, not law; by principles, not rules. When a person becomes a Christian, the Holy Spirit – God Himself – comes to live inside them. He gives the ability and strength to do what otherwise would be impossible. So, with the power and help of the Holy Spirit, a Christian is able to forgive, even in the most difficult of circumstances.

LEARNING FORGIVENESS

Jesus was asked by His disciple Peter how many times a person should forgive another. Peter then suggested that the answer was seven. Jesus replied that seven was not sufficient; seventy times seven was more like it. While Jesus quoted a certain and definite number, 'seventy times seven' is symbolic, meaning an uncertain and indefinite number – we are to forgive infinitely. He then told a parable to explain both the basis for our beliefs and behaviour.

The story was of a servant who owed his master a fortune, but when he couldn't pay, he begged for and received mercy. The master cancelled his debt. This forgiven man then tracked down a fellow-servant who owed him a tiny amount in comparison with the debt he had just had cancelled. Instead of listening to the pleas for mercy from his fellow-servant, the forgiven servant had his debtor thrown in prison. When the master heard the story of such callous treatment, he went to the servant, rebuked him, revoked the clearing of the debt, and had him thrown in prison until he could pay.[2]

The lessons are clear: all that every Christian has – namely forgiveness, peace with God and an eternal relationship with Him – is entirely due to the grace and goodness of God. In turn, gratitude should be the basis of the Christian's behaviour. Because God has forgiven us so much, we in turn should forgive others. Whatever they have done to us is no match to the way we have disregarded and rebelled against God. God has shown to the Christian mercy (not getting what we do deserve) and grace (getting what we do not deserve). If a person does not know God as a forgiving God, they will never know Him as the Father God. The responsibility for those who have been forgiven is that they will forgive others.

Of course, though, God does not glibly forgive; He forgives when there is repentance and sorrow for the wrong committed. While Christians will always want to forgive those who have wronged them, strictly speaking there can only be true forgiveness when someone is sorry for what they have done. Jesus said to His followers, 'If your brother sins against you, rebuke him; and if he repents, forgive him. And if he sins against you seven times in a day, and seven times in a day returns to you, saying, "I repent," you shall forgive him.'[3]

DEMONSTRATING GRACE

Demonstrating to others what she herself had received from God was what motivated Jo Pollard, whose husband, Michael, was murdered in Hungary. For thirty years, Michael and Jo, with their family, had taken humanitarian aid, medication, Bibles and Christian books into Communist Europe. They had experienced amazing answers to prayer, both in crossing the borders into the Communist bloc and travelling throughout those 'closed' countries.

Eight years after the 'Iron Curtain' had collapsed, and on their way to Ukraine with desperately needed provisions, they were robbed in a lay-by. Michael was bludgeoned to death and an attempt was made on Jo's life.

Three teenagers were later found guilty of murder, but, from a hospital bed in Hungary to the *ITV News* in the UK, Jo said she bore no malice. At Michael's funeral, she even sang as a solo the hymn 'How Great Thou Art'. She regularly prayed for the three men who had killed her husband. Later, she visited the jail in Hungary where the men were held. Two of the three prisoners were willing to meet her, where she told them that she forgave them, and presented them with small gifts. One of them has subsequently asked Christ for forgiveness.

To forgive was no mean task as Jo had not only lost her husband and the father of her three children, but has also suffered serious ill health since the attack. Jo was not minimising what had happened, but recognised that she too had received forgiveness, and now she could show it to these men.

AVOIDING BITTERNESS

Repeatedly, the Bible teaches that Christians should forgive. Jesus said, 'Blessed are the merciful, for they shall obtain mercy.'[4] The 'Lord's Prayer' – Jesus' model prayer – says, 'Forgive us our sins, for we also forgive everyone who sins against us.'[5] Even on the cross, Jesus prayed to His Father that there would be forgiveness for those responsible for His execution: 'Father, forgive them, for they do not know what they are doing.'[6] And the apostle Paul wrote to Christians in the church in Ephesus, 'Be kind and compassionate to one another, forgiving each another, just as in Christ God forgave you.'[7]

To forgive others is to do what we most want God to do for us. In being willing to receive God's forgiveness and willing to forgive others, it is right to forgive ourselves as well, otherwise we are setting ourselves as a higher judge than God Himself. Inability to forgive oneself is often based on the fear that we will commit the same sin again. The Holy Spirit can give the strength to overcome the things that dog us. As we learn to forgive ourselves, we consequently live at peace with ourselves even though we are conscious of past failures.

To forgive and to be forgiven is therapeutic. In contrast, to hold bitterness or resentment, to seek vengeance or to bear malice wears away at our innermost being; it distorts the image of joy and peace that one can see sometimes in a toddler or a young person. Better to forgive and let God avenge the wrong. He is merciful but absolutely just, so there are things best left in His hands.

We can have confidence that God, who instructs us to forgive, will give us the strength to do so – even when that may appear impossible because of an unwillingness to do as He commands. It was said of the sixteenth-century Archbishop Cranmer that if you did him an injury, he was sure to be your friend. Clearly he had cultivated obeying Jesus' command to love our enemies and pray for those who persecute us.

The first genocide of the twentieth century was against the Armenians. In 1915, over a million Armenians were driven to death in just six months. Thirty years later, and one week before the German invasion of Poland, Adolf Hitler said, 'Who, after all, speaks today of the annihilation of the Armenians?'[8] Rev. Sisag Manoogian lived through the genocide, experiencing thirty-three miraculous escapes from the Turks. He later wrote:

> *Thank God that many Armenians have been able, by the grace of God, to show that their spiritual life is nearer and dearer to them than material things. Some ferocious gendarmes marvelled when seeing men and women, even children, instead of trembling in the presence of death, show calm and dignity, and instead of cursing, pray for the forgiveness of their murderers.*[9]

Bitterness is dealt with by resetting our expectations. Giving our rights over to God deals a death blow to the bitterness which can spring up within. For example, a cancer patient may become bitter because they feel they have a right to good health. If instead they give that right to God, by praying and saying, 'Whether or not I have good health is in Your hands,' then there can be rest whatever lies ahead; they are accepting God's purpose for their life and can therefore be thankful rather than bitter. So Joseph, whose 'coat of many colours' was taken from him as he was sold into slavery by his brothers, could later say to them, 'You intended to harm me, but God intended it for good ...'[10]

CHAPTER 10

COMPASSION

The greatest world atrocity to have happened to date in my lifetime was the 1994 genocide in Rwanda. In the short space of 100 days, one tenth of the population of that African state were massacred. Deep-seated hatred between the Hutus and Tutsis ran riot as national radio whipped up support for the Hutu rebels, precipitating a mass murder of the Tutsis, and deaths of fighters on both sides.

The 2004 film *Hotel Rwanda* tells the true story of Paul Rusesabagina, manager of the prestigious Hotel des Mille Collines in Kigali. A Hutu, he had married a Tutsi. During the uprising, he used his position in the hotel, and his Hutu status, to shelter 1268 Tutsis from the savage killings taking place outside the hotel grounds. The film not only captures the intense psychological terror of the genocide, and the inability – or unwillingness – of the world's powers to intervene, but also one man's reaction to the horrors, evil and injustice around him. In times like this, individuals can demonstrate extraordinary strength and courage to stand up for and shelter the needy. Yet Christians in all situations are called on to step out of their comfort zones, to respond to injustice and to show compassion.

RESPONDING TO INJUSTICE

In 'first-world countries' it is easy for Christians to hold strong beliefs, and to focus on their own needs, while ignoring the plight of millions living on the same planet as them. There are many moral and social issues which lead to political campaigns, but though they may be worthy causes, one cannot wonder if their concerns are out of balance; they campaign for these issues from lovely houses in leafy suburbs while millions barely survive in abject poverty.

One of the great transformations to take place when someone truly comes to know Jesus Christ personally is that their view of the world is altered. For one, they become part of a global family, with 'brothers and sisters' around the globe. A nomadic family living in northern Mongolia; single people working in the financial districts of Tokyo, New York, London and Sydney; a remote tribe in the jungle in Papua New Guinea; and a young couple trying to survive in a shanty town in Honduras: all these can be united as followers of Jesus Christ, and part of His worldwide family, the church.

The Hutu and Tutsi conflict that ravaged Rwanda also engulfed other African countries during the mid-1990s, including Burundi. Fighting broke out on the university campus, and a number of Hutu students were killed; others fled to nearby mountains. They were followed by Tutsi Christians who took food and clothing first to their Christian 'brothers and sisters', but also to others. Some of these Tutsi students were later rejected by their families because they put their allegiance to fellow believers in Jesus Christ ahead of tribal allegiance. However, the Principal of the university, who did not call himself a Christian, said on record, 'Our culture is disintegrating. On our campus there are three types of people: Hutus, Tutsis and Christians. If our culture is to survive, we must follow the examples of the Christians.'[1]

One of the characteristics of this worldwide church 'family' is that we have a desire, and a responsibility, to care for our brothers and sisters who are in need. This might mean effort to talk to a fellow Christian even if they are not one's 'type', or caring for a recent widow, or providing meals for students at church to save them from another beans-on-toast dinner or pasta salad. It might, on the other hand, mean giving a few weeks, or months or even years to offer practical and spiritual support to Christian brothers and sisters in Uganda, or Afghanistan, or Lima or inner-city Liverpool.

SHOWING COMPASSION

A belief that God is ultimately good and in control does not mean that Christians can sit back and relax. The Old Testament prophets had renounced the ungodliness of nations which neglected the needs of orphans, widows, immigrants and the poor. The prophet Micah had said that God 'has shown you, O man, what is good; and what does the Lord require of you but to do justly, to love mercy and to walk humbly with your God?'[2]

Jesus Himself was moved with compassion when He saw people who were like 'sheep without a shepherd'.[3] He healed the sick, giving sight to the blind, hearing to the deaf, speech to the mute, strength to the lame and paralysed, and even life to the dead. He fed hungry crowds, cured people with leprosy, cast out demons from the tormented, and met the spiritual needs of those who came to Him. He worked and taught, and trained His disciples to do the same. He went about doing good. He cared for the underdogs, the neglected and the needy, taking time with those others ignore.

His followers have sought to follow His example. Early in church history, Christians sold what they had and distributed their goods to the poor. Collections were taken to give to the poor and people who had suffered because of famine. Jesus' disciple John wrote to Christians saying, 'If anyone has material possessions and sees a brother or sister in need but has no pity on him, how can the love of God be in that person? Dear children, let us not love with words or speech but with actions and in truth.'[4]

There is an inner compulsion in followers of Christ, as well as direct commands to do so, that leads them to commit to hard work in physical, social and spiritual ways. For example, during the period of social reform in the eighteenth century, it was the evangelical community that worked for the abolition of slavery, medical provision, the establishment of orphanages, and the reform of child labour and prison abuses. Christians have been at the forefront of establishing schools, health care and hospitals throughout the world. Others have given their lives to guarantee free speech, to alleviate suffering and to proclaim the good news of Jesus who said that He had come 'to proclaim good news to the poor … to proclaim freedom for the prisoners and recovery of sight for the blind, to set the oppressed free …'[5]

I admire Nelson Mandela's lack of bitterness and selfless leadership shown upon his release from prison. In his autobiography, he describes a touching incident which happened in the dark years, as he calls them, of his time in jail on Robben Island. It occurred shortly after he had heard of his wife, Winnie, being imprisoned:

During this time I experienced another grievous loss. One cold morning in July of 1969, three months after I learned of Winnie's incarceration, I was called to the main office on Robben Island and handed a telegram. It was from my youngest son, Makgatho, and it was only a sentence long. He informed me that his older brother, my first and oldest son, Madiba Thembekile, whom we called Thembi, had been killed in a motorcar accident in the Transkei. Thembi was then twenty-five-years old, and the father of two small children.

What can I say about such a tragedy? I was overwrought about my wife, I was still grieving for my mother, and then to hear such news … I do not have words to express the sorrow, or the loss I felt. It left a hole in my heart that can never be filled.

I returned to my cell and lay on my bed. I do not know how long I stayed there, but I did not emerge for dinner. Some of the men looked in, but I said nothing. Finally, Walter came to me and knelt beside my bed, and I handed him the telegram. He said nothing, but only held my hand. I do not know how long he remained with me. There is nothing one man can say to another at such a time.[6]

I admire the silent compassion of Walter demonstrated in a prison cell to a man who seemed to have lost everything. It reminds me of Jesus freely touching ostracised lepers, or His tender words to an unrecognised widow who generously gave money that others would have discarded. Compassion should be a hallmark of Christians, and we can learn much from the example of Jesus and of individuals like Walter in South Africa and Paul Rusesabagina in Rwanda.

CHAPTER 11

ACCEPTANCE

Pain is not always dramatic or headline hitting. It might even be something one suffers alone; a hurt one carries around that is too painful to share with others. Loneliness, fear, poor self-image and rejection can hurt deep and sharp, and it's easy to think that no-one cares or understands.

American lyricist and singer Janis Ian captured the sentiments of many in her hit single 'At Seventeen':

> *To those of us who knew the pain*
> *Of valentines that never came*
> *And those whose names were never called*
> *When choosing sides for basketball*
> *It was long ago and far away*
> *The world was younger than today*
> *When dreams were all they gave for free*
> *To ugly duckling girls like me*

We all play the game, and when we dare
To cheat ourselves at solitaire
Inventing lovers on the phone
Repenting other lives unknown
That call and say – come dance with me
And murmur vague obscenities
At ugly girls like me, at seventeen.[1]

BEING IMPERFECT IN A 'PERFECT' WORLD

We live in a fallen, broken world which is obsessed with an unspoiled, perfect image. Whether finances, looks, career, relationships, intelligence, holidays, property, cars or talent, our world is consumed by success. Values are being squeezed out of society, while image has become all-important. If you don't make the grade, you're out; this world has no place for losers.

But wait! Whose world is this? Who rules the world? Does the world really belong to the rich and famous, to celebrities or powerful politicians? Do the media *really* control the direction this world is taking? It's easy to believe the answer to these questions is a resounding 'yes'. The reality, though, is that the true ruler of the world isn't swung by the size of one's wallet, or the number of letters after one's name. The true ruler of the world loves 'ugly duckling girls', as much as those on the front of celebrity magazines. He is not ageist, sexist or racist, but loves each person on this earth – past, present and future – as if His own. He longs for each one to be reconciled to Himself. This isn't a throwaway line. He sent His only Son so that each person on earth could be rescued, and brought into relationship with Him; a relationship that is based on us not being perfect and on us not deserving anything, but instead through which we are made 'perfect' and receive everything. God, the ruler of the earth, longs to be with the lonely, to comfort the grieving, to calm the fearful, to embrace those with low self-esteem, and to welcome the rejected. He has promised His companionship, and one can be sure that He will guide, guard and satisfy in a way that nothing or no-one else can.

LIVING WITH FEAR

Memories of the past so often haunt people, but then the future sometimes does too. There can be the deep-seated fear that there will never again be happiness, companionship or purpose to life. We can do nothing about the past, and even the future is largely out of our control, but we can adjust our attitudes to today, with transforming effects. Jesus addressed this issue when He said:

> … *do not worry about your life, what you will eat or drink; or about your body, what you will wear. Is not life more than food, and the body more important than clothes? Look at the birds of the air; they do not sow or reap or store away in barns, and yet your heavenly Father feeds them. Are you not much more valuable than they? Can any one of you by worrying add a single hour to your life?*

And why do you worry about clothes? See how the flowers of the field grow. They do not labour or spin. Yet I tell you that not even Solomon in all his splendour was dressed like one of these ... So do not worry, saying, 'What shall we eat?' or 'What shall we drink?' or 'What shall we wear?' ... But seek first [God's] kingdom and [God's] righteousness, and all these things will be given to you as well. Therefore, do not worry about tomorrow, for tomorrow will worry about itself. Each day has enough trouble of its own.[2]

Worry is like a fog, where millions of minute globules of water dim the vision of the way ahead. It is useless, needless and godless if we can have a trust in God that leaves us confident in His purposes. I have found that worry can be overcome. This comes about through recognising that we cannot deal with the issues that trouble us, but that we can give our concerns to God, leaving them in His control. If the worry continues to nag away, we remind ourselves that God is dealing with the problem. It is practising what we read in the psalms: 'Cast your burden on the Lord and He shall sustain you'.[3]

FINDING STRENGTH

C.S. Lewis, the famed author of *The Lion, the Witch and the Wardrobe*, expressed wryly the common Christian attitude in one of his letters: 'We are not necessarily doubting that God will do the best for us; we are wondering how painful the best will turn out to be.'[4] This is certainly true when facing death. We know our future after death is certain, but before this we may go through a terrible time of pain and suffering.

Sometimes, the weight of the world and life's difficulties can be so heavy that we cannot imagine a way of making it through without crumbling. However, the Creator God loves us and gives hope to those who put their confidence in Him. Suffering is so draining, but God's strength is eternal, and there to be tapped. Isaiah, a prophet who lived around 700 bc, wrote some words, which were famously read by Eric Liddell's character in the film *Chariots of Fire*:

> *The Lord is the everlasting God,*
> *the Creator of the ends of the earth.*
> *He will not grow tired or weary,*
> *and [His] understanding no-one can fathom.*
> *He gives strength to the weary*
> *and increases the power of the weak.*
> *Even youths grow tired and weary,*
> *and young men stumble and fall;*
> *but those who hope in the Lord*
> *will renew their strength.*
> *They will soar on wings like eagles;*
> *they will run and not grow weary,*
> *they will walk and not be faint.*[5]

While our bodies may fail, our spirits be crushed and our minds falter, we can find new sources of energy and strength in God. He can give us the resources we need, not necessarily to escape the circumstances we are in, but to cope, and even to 'soar' in situations where we felt we were sinking.

ACCEPTING UNKNOWNS

I have often heard people talk about faith in a mystical way, particularly when it comes to suffering. For example, someone shares they have terminal cancer, and they receive the reply: 'Well, it's a good thing you have faith.' Or a person dies, and friends say, 'At least they had a strong faith.' What is wrong about this view of 'faith' is that it is seen as a magic charm, or a good-luck mascot. In reality, the most important aspect of faith is the *focus* of the faith – who or what the faith is in. Misplaced faith is as good as no faith at all.

Faith in God is based on the truth of who He is and how He has demonstrated Himself. It is not a 'blind faith', but a faith based on facts and experience. We don't know everything about God, as His very nature as God means we cannot possibly understand everything about Him. However, we can trust in His character and His promises. As we witness how He has demonstrated Himself in the past, and worked in our own lives, we can learn to trust Him for the unknowns.

We don't always know if we will be healed from an illness, rescued from death, enjoy long-lasting relationships, keep our job, be free from natural disaster, or have enough resources to live on; yet we can trust that God is in control – of the world, and of our own day-today lives. He has not left us alone. In fact, He has gone to great lengths to ensure there is a way that we can one day be free of this world and its problems, enjoying the world as He intended it to be.

I know I often struggle with this as I like to keep 'control'. The idea of submitting oneself to someone else, even if that 'someone' be God, is most unappealing. But if we do, we find that the dreaded unknowns can be placed in God's hands and we can rest assured that He will take care of us – whatever the future holds.

Dr Steve Brady, when he was the Principal of a Christian college in England, made a similar point based on these words of Jesus: 'You do not realise now what I am doing, but later you will understand.' [6]With a wife suffering from multiple sclerosis and mounting family difficulties, Steve drew three straightforward conclusions from Jesus' words: be glad for what you do know; be humble for what you do not know; and be patient for what you will one day know.[7]

Such an attitude in no way excuses a fatalistic approach to life. *Que sera, sera,* ('whatever will be, will be') may have been a hit song in the fifties, but it is not good theology. We have the role model of Jesus who 'went about doing good',[8] healing the sick, raising the dead, comforting the bereaved and welcoming the outcasts. Like Him, Christians should always do what is right, working to better the world around them.

Christians rightly pray for good health. The apostle John wrote to his friend Gauis saying, 'Dear friend, I pray that you may enjoy good health and that all may go well with you, just as you are progressing spiritually.'[9] We pray for protection and help in all situations. The litany in the Anglican Book of Common Prayer includes prayer 'from lightening and tempest; from plague, pestilence, and famine; from battle and murder, and from sudden death, Good Lord, deliver us.'[10]

Christians will work and strive to prevent disaster in this fallen world, and to help the weak and suffering, using legitimate means to bring about social and economic good. The disenfranchised and downtrodden should be able to experience just economic empowerment and social mobility. The Bible declares that God decries social and economic injustices; after all, He is a just God. Nevertheless, despite our aims, we will always have injustice because we live in a world that has not yet been put right by the Ruler of all, who will one day reign in justice and equity. Co-existing with our striving for justice is rest in knowing that God, who rules, also overrules in the situations we would naturally avoid at all costs.

CONCLUSION: FINDING GOD IN A MESSED-UP WORLD

Over twenty centuries ago, the region of Palestine was rocked by two tragedies. The first was a deliberate act of terrorism, instigated by Pilate and his men, in which a group of Galileans were killed while they worshipped God. In the second incident, eighteen people died when an edifice, called the Tower of Siloam, collapsed and crushed them. In the same way that we ask the question 'why?' when we hear of deliberate or accidental tragedies, people asked the same question to Jesus two millennia ago. Despite the passage of time, the Bible is always relevant and topical, and we can learn directly from Jesus' response to these incidents.

We read of these events in the Gospel of Luke:

Now there were some present at that time who told Jesus about the Galileans whose blood Pilate had mixed with their sacrifices. Jesus answered, 'Do you think that these Galileans were worse sinners than all the other Galileans because they suffered this way? I tell you, no! But unless you repent, you too will all perish. Or those eighteen who died when the tower in Siloam fell on them – do you think they were more guilty than all the others living in Jerusalem? I tell you, no! But unless you repent, you too will all perish.[1]

A DESIRE TO TALK ABOUT DISASTER AND DEATH

We can see that there is often a desire to talk about disaster and death. Although in Britain, since the sixties, death has replaced sex as the big taboo subject, there is still an inclination to talk about death and disaster, even if not on a personal level. Following the Boxing Day tsunami in Asia, a friend commented to me that the reaction of friends in London was almost competitive – trying to show who was most 'moved' by what had happened. Although that might be a little cynical, it does indicate an attitude. We love to talk and debate about the tragedies we're witnessing around us; our news wouldn't be dominated by such dreadful stories if there wasn't appetite for them. In the same way, these disasters wouldn't have been raised with Jesus had people not wanted to discuss them.

When people are confronted by nationwide troubles, city-wide disaster or close suffering, there is a stirring in hearts and questioning in minds. Often there is an expression, in the best way people are able, of their sympathy and compassion. There is nothing wrong with grief. Jesus wept at the tomb of His friend Lazarus who had died, even though He was to raise him back to life when he had been dead for four whole days. However, a place of disaster has the danger of being turned into a 'pagan shrine'. Grief can bring about a mixture of sentiment, superstition and falsehood. Out of desperation for comfort and answers, there can be a tendency to cling onto anything that offers hope, whether true or false.

A NEED TO LEARN FROM DISASTERS

We can also see that there is a need to learn from disaster. We want to know if it could have been prevented, and if so, who is to blame and what can be done to avoid such a thing in the future.

Jesus responded to this need, and spoke about the reason for such events. In the case of the murder and martyrdom of the Galilean worshippers, the cause was straightforward: human evil. Pilate's cruelty led to the death of innocent victims. So it was when two planes ploughed into the Twin Towers on 11 September 2001, or when the Kurds were gassed and Marsh Arabs killed by Saddam Hussein's men. The sinfulness of an individual or group led to the suffering and death of hundreds of others.

In contrast, when the Tower of Siloam fell, it was not a specific act of violence, but rather a tragic accident. We are part of the world and all too often caught up in its tragedies. Blame sometimes cannot be laid at the feet of anybody in particular.

In both cases, Jesus taught that one must not judge people's sins by their present sufferings. The men and women who died were neither more innocent nor more sinful than others. As Jesus also said concerning a man who had been born blind, it was neither the sin of the man nor his parents that has caused his blindness, 'but this happened so that the works of God might be displayed in him.'[2]

In the discussion about the massacre of the Galileans and the collapse of the Tower of Siloam, Jesus moved the conversation to focus on another lesson we need to learn from disaster and death: the need to repent. Twice he said, '… unless you repent, you too will all perish.'

John the Baptist, the cousin of Jesus who prepared the way for His coming, had as his great theme 'repent'. Jesus' disciple Peter preached the first 'Christian' sermon; its theme was 'repent'. Paul, the man who carried the Christian message throughout the then-known world, continually stressed in his messages, 'repent'. Here too, God Himself calls people to 'repent'.

To repent means a change of heart, mind and ways. It is a turning from one's own ways, trusting that these can be completely forgiven because of what Jesus did on the cross, and accepting His loving rule and guidance of your life. Repentance is the only way of escaping judgement. The Christian faith is not just a set of beliefs; it is about a complete transformation.

Jonah, an Old Testament prophet, preached that the city of Nineveh would be destroyed in forty days. All the people in Nineveh repented and God was merciful to the vast city. The wicked King Mannasseh, of whom we also read in the Bible, burned his own children as a sacrifice to false gods and led the people of Judah into idolatry and immorality, but repented and God was merciful to him.[3]

Britain at the beginning of the eighteenth century was noted for its debauchery and drunkenness, but through the preaching of an enthusiastic group of evangelists, including John Wesley and George Whitefield, many in Britain experienced a complete transformation, and again God was merciful. This led to a great social awareness in the land. Christian people – such as William Wilberforce (who worked for the abolition of slavery); Lord Shaftesbury (who brought about factory and child-labour reform); and John Howard and Elizabeth Fry (who worked for prison reform) – began to campaign tirelessly to alleviate social injustice and suffering.

Today, we also need to repent of our sins. It might appear old-fashioned, or completely alien to us, but we all know there are things that are not right in the way we live, think, speak and act. Each of us must turn from sin and renounce it, and turn to Christ to receive us.

A RIGHT ATTITUDE TO DEVELOP CONCERNING DEATH AND DISASTER

We see from this incident in Luke chapter13 that there is a right attitude to develop concerning death and disaster. The 'Troubles' in Northern Ireland were a running sore in the United Kingdom in the latter part of the twentieth century. Mingled in the sadness and tragedy were many incidents of faith and courage. For example, Bill McConnell was the deputy governor of the notorious Maze Prison. He was murdered in front of his wife, Beryl, and three-year-old daughter, Gail.

Bill had had a premonition of death three weeks before his murder. He wrote a letter to be read at his funeral. It was also published in national newspapers. The last paragraph read:

> *Finally, let no one be alarmed as to my eternal security. [Years ago], I committed my life, talents, work and actions to Almighty God in sure and certain knowledge that however slight my hold upon Him may have been during my years at school, university and the prison service, His promises are sure, and His hold on me complete. Nothing can separate me from the love of God in Christ Jesus our Lord.*

Do you have such confidence in the face of death? Death is inescapable and, though we never know in advance, it could be imminent. The Tower of Siloam was built for safety, but it proved to be the place of people's death.

Peter Marshall was a greatly respected chaplain to the American senate. He used to tell this story:

> *An old legend tells of a merchant in Baghdad who one day sent his servant to the market. Before very long the servant came back, pale and trembling. In great agitation he said to his master, 'Down in the marketplace I was jostled by a woman in the crowd, and when I turned around I saw it was Death. She looked at me and made a threatening gesture. Master, please lend me your horse, for I must hasten to avoid her. I will ride to Samarra and there I will hide and Death will not find me.'*
>
> *The merchant lent him his horse and the servant galloped away in great haste. Later the merchant went down to the market and saw Death standing in the crowd. He asked her, 'Why did you frighten my servant this morning? Why did you make a threatening gesture?'*
>
> *'That was not a threatening gesture,' Death said. 'It was only a start of surprise. I was astonished to see him in Baghdad, for I have an appointment with him tonight in Samarra!'*[4]

Whether our life ends slowly or suddenly, each person will eventually stand before God. It is easy to laugh at the characters who distribute Christian leaflets, or hold up banners with Bible sentences or dramatic phrases. However, outside the Hillsborough football ground in Sheffield on the fateful Saturday when ninety-six fans died, Keith Bowers of Morecambe had prayed concerning which banners and leaflets he should carry and hand out to the crowds. The banner he decided on, and held up to thousands of football supporters, displayed the words: 'Prepare to meet your God.' They could not have been more relevant.

A GOD TO TRUST IN PREPARATION FOR DISASTER AND DEATH

The passage in Luke's Gospel also contains some good news. We see that there is a God to trust in preparation for possible disaster and certain death. Jesus repeatedly warns us of the vital, urgent need to repent. He is patient, but His warning still applies.

Early in Genesis, the first book of the Bible, we read the story of Noah building a giant boat, or ark, of safety before the world's first major catastrophe: a destructive flood. For 120 years, Noah built while preaching to the people who worked for him to warn them of impending judgement, and explaining that the ark was the way of escape. Even when he, his family and selected animals had entered the ark, God kept its door open for seven more days. It was a silent sermon and invitation for everyone to enter. Eventually, God Himself shut the door. The time of invitation and the opportunity for the people to repent was over, for ever.

For two thousand years, the command to repent and Jesus' invitation, 'Come to me, all you who are weary and burdened, and I will give you rest,'⁵ have been declared. God will eventually 'close the door' and then it will be too late. 'I tell you,' said Jesus, '… unless you repent, you too will all perish.' Our 'perishing' will be eternal. To be cut off from God in conscious, eternal punishment is a terrible thing. Yet God is compassionate. As the Bible says, 'For God so loved the world that He gave His only begotten Son, that whoever believes in Him should not perish but have everlasting life.'⁶

Sometimes in funeral services one can get the impression that everyone will go to heaven and be alright after death. Jesus made it very clear that that is not so. Our sin would keep us out of heaven. To be sure of eternal life, we must make sure that our sin has been forgiven and that we are in a right relationship with God.

Christ's death was not an accident. It was God's plan that Jesus should come and lay down His life. It was to be humanity's only hope. Sin always brings death – either the death of the sinner, or the death of a substitute. Christ died as a substitute for us. Our sin was laid on Him and He took all our guilt so that we might be forgiven. Christ's death was not a disaster, but was the greatest act of love that the world has seen. What looked like a terrible tragedy actually was God demonstrating His great love towards us.

In fact, the death and rising again of the Lord Jesus was God's greatest work. God was reconciling the world to Himself in Christ, not counting people's sin against them. Sins committed from the beginning of time, through the ages and to the end of time were all focused onto Jesus Christ. He became sin for us. Sin always carries a penalty, but Christ paid for it in our place.

Having died for us, He was buried in a sealed, previously unused tomb in a garden. Three days later, Jesus rose from the dead. He overcame the things that overcome us, namely sin and death. Through His death and resurrection, Jesus has opened the way so that we may now be forgiven and enjoy God, through His Holy Spirit, living in our hearts, minds and lives. As soon as a person turns from their own direction and asks Jesus to be their Lord, Saviour and Friend, a relationship with God begins, which will last throughout life and on through eternity.

Time is short, but so are memories. I recently stood at the scene of the fire which tore through a nightclub in Rhode Island in 2003. Ninety-eight people died in the inferno, but the world has largely forgotten this tragedy. In contrast, Jesus Christ's death has not been forgotten. Significantly, Christians regularly gather in a ceremony where they eat bread and drink a little wine to deliberately remember that Jesus died for them. Just as the bread is broken to be eaten, Jesus' body was broken when He was crucified. As the wine is sipped, so Jesus' blood was spilt as He suffered on the cross to buy for us forgiveness and new life. We can never forget such a sacrifice.

Christ's death was not the last that we saw of Him. Jesus defeated the grave. He rose again from the dead! Having beaten sin and death, He ascended to heaven. The Bible teaches that, one day, Jesus will return to be acknowledged as the King of kings and Lord of lords. The oft-repeated prayer, 'Your kingdom come' will be answered and Christ will establish His reign on earth.

A BIGGER DISASTER TO AVOID

There is a bigger disaster to avoid than the ones which sadly hit the headlines. Perhaps the most tragic word in the English language is the word 'lost'. That is why it is imperative to trust Jesus as your Saviour. We each need to answer this question: 'Have I asked Jesus Christ to forgive me and to live within me?'

Will you now ask God to forgive your past, guide your present and be with you forever? There is a degree of urgency about that question. We never know what the future may bring. I wonder whether part of the awfulness of being lost from God is the sense of regret: that God was so close, and yet was neglected or refused. In the Old Abbey Kirk at Haddington, in Scotland, one can read over the grave of Jane Welsh one of many pathetic and regretful tributes paid by Thomas Carlyle to his neglected wife: 'For forty years she was a true and loving helpmate of her husband, and by act and work worthily forwarded me as none else could … She died at London the 21st of April, 1866, suddenly snatched from him, and the light of his life as if gone out.'[7]

It has been said that the saddest sentence in English literature is this sentence written by Carlyle in his diary: 'Oh, that I had you yet for five minutes by my side, that I might tell you all.'

Although the Christian cannot answer every question concerning faith in Christ and all that is going on in the world, Christians know God. They have believed in Him, and are convinced that He will keep them throughout life, through death and for eternity. The Bible says, 'Everyone who calls on the name of the Lord will be saved.'⁸ There is no need to have regrets; the offer of forgiveness and new, eternal life is open to all.

I would encourage you to pray, to talk to God, and tell Him where you are at in your thinking. Share your feelings about your own personal struggles or troubles in the world. Ask Him to forgive you for all that is wrong, for not following Him and His ways. Ask Him to come to live within you and, by the power of His Holy Spirit, to be your Lord, Saviour and Friend. As you trust Him like this, ask Him to give you the strength to follow Him. Sharing, worshipping and serving God with other Christians will be immense benefit to you as you start to grow in your faith, and cultivate your relationship with God.

As you live for Him, you will find the privilege of getting to know God here on earth. One day in heaven, we will begin to understand better the things that have puzzled us now.

DEPRESSION: A PERSONAL POINT OF VIEW

I am not a doctor, psychologist or psychiatrist, but I have been a patient. What I share is simply one person's journey with depression, but I do not pretend to be a medical expert or to understand the workings of the mind. However, like every other individual, I battle against human frailty of one sort or another. For some people, that may mean the limitation of physical weakness; for others, it can be emotional or mental hurdles that may seem insurmountable.

I understand depression to be when the inward mental and emotional structure that normally is intrinsic to our human existence weakens, crumbles or becomes distorted. Depression can affect anyone and can happen at any time, but certain personality types are more prone to it. Types of depression vary from mild mood changes to clinical depression or manic depression, with its 'ups' and its 'downs'. Depression can be triggered by a crisis such as death, divorce, redundancy or deep disappointment, or depression can develop in the mind of someone who otherwise appears to be well and in control of life. When I have been depressed, it is hard to remember what it feels like to be well, and when I am well, it is difficult to recall just how it felt to be sick.

What I have been through is a common enough experience, and though it has been terrible, I am aware of many who have much more serious times of suffering.

MY PERSONAL EXPERIENCE

I have always regarded myself as a fairly cheerful and, at times, mischievous character. However, I recall talking one sunny summer with a pastor about depression soon after becoming a Christian – when I was just sixteen years old. Clearly, there has been an issue with depression within me for a long time. I am drawn to melancholic music, books and paintings. From teenage years, I have been an intermittent insomniac as well, who works late nights, but then finds it difficult to sleep. I love my work, and can be a workaholic. I don't find it easy to 'switch off' or rest, and rarely have a break. And then, speaking personally, I can be a sensitive soul who feels deeply for the hurts of others, and it is not easy to shake off the thoughts of what others are suffering. I take these things to heart, and they remain there, gnawing away at me.

Some years ago, I began to find certain aspects of my work overwhelming. Every phone call – and we had three telephone lines coming into our home, and then a mobile phone – seemed too much for me; I couldn't cope with inconsequential chatter, or even the laughter of others. I became annoyed even when people asked me to speak somewhere (which, of course, is my life's work!), wishing people would just leave me alone. I was walking an emotional tightrope, and finding myself easily falling off and plunging into the safety net of tears and sobbing; yet I couldn't put a finger on the reason why.

As a Christian, I searched my heart to see if there was any sin I was clinging to that was coming between God and me. While not claiming to be sinless, I sincerely believed that all my sins were covered by Christ's death on the cross and that there was nothing hindering my relationship with Him. Jesus had died paying the penalty of my wrong, and I was trusting in the crucified, now risen Christ as my Lord and Saviour. I loved Him with all my heart and longed to see others coming to a saving faith in Him too.

A doctor friend talked with me and advised me to take a sabbatical, and so I set about cancelling various future appointments to give myself a four-month break. (Looking back, that period became sick leave rather than a sabbatical, which I have still never managed to have!) By the time that four-month period had arrived, my state of mind had deteriorated. I was beginning to sink into a depth of great, inward darkness. I did not want to talk with anyone. I continued to read the Bible, pray and go to church, but avoided talking with people at the end of the service.

My mind was telling me things that were not true. The depression affected my perception of things, so that I had a distorted point of view. For some time, I had thought I would collapse while preaching in the pulpit. I believed nobody cared whether I lived or died. I went to bed each evening hoping I would die in the night, and would wake up the next day feeling I could not face the hours ahead. However, I never doubted God, even in my lowest moments. I was convinced that God was in control of all that was going on, and that He would not waste any time, pain, tears or toil of mine. I am aware that others struggle with doubts, which compound their suffering, but that was not my experience.

As well as talking with my very understanding family doctor, I went to a psychologist, who felt that if I could learn to breathe more slowly and take life more gently, I would be better. My doctor was keen for me to see a professional counsellor, but I did not want to talk to anyone else. To suffer alone was itself too much for me, without the added burden of speaking to someone I did not know. Every conversation added to the inward pain and hurt. I felt that any meaningful explanation of the complexities of my mind and life would demand of me more than I felt able to give.

Many people wrote or sent cards assuring me of their prayers, each of which was appreciated. Two friends in particular wrote at length, and one (helpfully) insisted on visiting me. Both assured me that I would eventually come through the depression. Although I felt there was no future, the fact that two people wrote the same thing, giving a more positive view of the future, was very encouraging. I had yet to learn that today is not forever. I have reread those letters many times and they have proved to be a repeated source of encouragement.

There were others who hurt a little with their glib comments, such as: 'Snap out of it' (I would have given my right arm to have been able to do that!), or 'Been there, done that.' Each one caused pain, but no doubt they meant well. For me, their comments led to more tears. God never spoke to my heart through them, or in that way.

I remember how on one occasion my son simply put his arm around me when he found me crying in my study. It was a moment of great comfort to me. Being hugged is part of being healed.

SUICIDE

Although I don't drink alcohol, in the darkness of my depression I wanted to get drunk. I thought that if I was drunk, at least for an evening I would not feel the tangible, emotional pain that was within. That pain is just as real as toothache. It makes darkness more preferable to light. As a friend of mine wrote to me, 'It gives the impression that "the sun is laughing at you".' This pain can deprive us of pleasures that we formerly took for granted. Time and again I have empathised with the last words of Vincent van Gogh: '*La tristesse durea,*' which means, 'The sadness will never go away.'

As a result of depression being about a loss of well-being, thoughts of dying dominated my mind. All human beings think about death at times, but now there was a craving for death. I knew that suicide is always wrong; it is not natural, and it is a breaking of God's commandment. God, who is the giver of life, says we are not to take life, even our own; it is self-murder. As well, it transfers the pain to the innocent family members who are left. Yet I knew also that it is not an unforgivable sin, and at one particularly low time, I meticulously planned my 'accidental death'. I didn't want to cause God's enemies to blaspheme His name, so I planned a suicide that I was sure would be recorded as accidental death. I cannot tell you how near I was to taking my own life, but refrained from doing so because I felt it would scar the life of my wife and four children until their dying day. Perversely, minutes before the dreadful moment of 'death', I was talking with a non-Christian about Jesus, longing that he too would come to know Christ, while at the same time intending to take my own life.

One of the Christian friends who wrote to me firmly grasped the nettle regarding my thoughts of suicide. In his letter, he explained how depression can really be anger turned inwards, and so becomes self-destructive. Of course, there are instances in the Bible that can illustrate this. For example, Judas was angry with himself for what he had done in betraying Jesus, found no solace in seeking to return the money he had made, and so went out and took his own life. If anger is related to the depression, then we must ask ourselves, 'With whom are we angry?' It could be a person, group, God, ourselves or the situation we are in. Anger and prayer do not go together, for we read we should be '… lifting up holy hands [i.e. praying to God] without anger… '[1] Therefore, before God, we have to deal with our anger and be totally honest about how we feel.

The Book of Psalms was a great blessing to me.[2] Repeatedly, I found that the psalmist had experienced just what I was feeling. There are many examples where the psalmist imaginatively describes his troubles as waves of sorrow which were overtaking him. Yet we also find the psalmist speaking to himself and reminding his innermost being of God's blessings in the past and promises for the future. Psalms 42 and 43 are good examples of this. In the psalms, we read of anger, disappointment, frustrations, joy, relief, wonderment and the sense of being let down. The exercise of stepping outside ourselves and posing a question to oneself is not easy, but is demonstrated in the Bible and can be rewarding and helpful. When times are very dark, it is good to be able to assure oneself that 'God is going to get me through this' and that, with His help, we can glorify God through this experience.

RECOVERY

With the passage of many months, I was beginning to recover, though still feeling pained. Throughout my sick leave, I had been working on the manuscript of a book.

I went back to work and resumed speaking publicly and mixing with others, but I was still struggling. While having a meal with a pastor, I again began to cry. He recommended that I go to see a particular Christian psychiatrist in London, which I did. I remember so clearly the psychiatrist saying that I was sick, but that he could help me.

This promise of help meant the world to me. I had already tried three different types of drugs, two of which proved of no help, and one of which did strange things to my mind, and rather unwisely I abruptly stopped taking it. This caused further traumas to my mind. He put me on an older type of drug, and gradually this seemed to work as it drew me out of my depression.

As a Christian, I am sure it is not at all wrong to be on medication. The world has been wrecked, and this includes physical and mental effects on our beings. As I would not hesitate to take medication if I was physically sick, so I was willing to take medication for my mind. There are, though, side effects to drugs, which I experienced. However, these were preferable to the pain I had been experiencing.

Eventually … slowly … erratically … I came out of that dreadful bout of depression. I still need to learn to be patient with myself as recovery is very gradual, and I am still trying to understand what was happening to me.

SUFFERING AND GLORY

In 1 Peter and elsewhere in the Bible, we read that both suffering and glory characterise the Christian life.

The Christian is not immune from normal sicknesses. However, we can be sure that God does not forget us in any situation, and He is well able to heal – if that is His purpose. God never wastes any tears. He never wastes any pain. And we can trust that He will use what we experience for good. Depression recurred a few years after, but with new medication prescribed by another Christian psychiatrist, I came through another desperately dark time. It is now many years since those awful times, though, of course, emotions can still take me to the heights but also the depths.

So, what have I learnt through this period?

I learnt that there are benefits in buffetings! I have found a fresh confidence in God. Because my mind was telling me things that were not true, I sought to speak to my innermost being and remind myself of 'true truth'. This is what the psalmist does in Psalm 42. For example, we read:

Why are you cast down, O my soul?
And why are you disquieted within me?
Hope in God, for I shall yet praise Him
For the help of His countenance.[3]

The psalmist spoke truth to his soul and questioned its disturbed state. I had to remind myself of God's love towards me, of how He has blessed and helped in the past, and of what He promises in the future. It was also good to know that Jesus, who Himself was called 'a Man of sorrows',[4] cared and could cope.

In Isaiah 45, we read that God says:

I will give you the treasures of darkness
And hidden riches of secret places,
That you may know that I, the Lord,
Who call you by your name,
Am the God of Israel.[5]

In the darkness and despair of depression, as I felt I was sinking ever deeper, God gave treasures. I experienced God's love and tender, therapeutic care. I am certainly aware of my own vulnerability in a way I had not recognised before, and I believe I have a more compassionate view towards those who suffer mental illness; before I was quite dispassionate towards mental weakness. This was an important thing for me to learn, because as Christians we will want to have compassion on those whose physical and mental strength has collapsed. There is no stigma in having mental illness such as depression; there is no blame attached – just as there is none to someone suffering from flu, cancer or a broken leg.

I am aware that depression could recur for me. Frankly, I fear it happening again and would not wish the inward darkness on anyone, but I am also aware that God works all things together for my good and His glory. He is God and is in control, and whatever the future holds, God can renew and keep me.

HELPFUL BIBLE VERSES

The Book of Psalms is the Bible's song book. It is found right in the middle of the Bible and contains 150 Psalms which express to God every human emotion. It is impossible to summarise them, but they teach that though life is tough, God is good.

They have been a source of comfort to millions of God's people. Personally, I have repeatedly turned to them. I have found they express better than I ever could what is going on in my mind, but simultaneously point me to God who never fails to help.

When downhearted, discouraged or disappointed, the psalms are a good place to turn for comfort. When battling with pain, death or loss, seek God as you read the psalms. Here are some psalms to turn to in times of trouble:

Psalm 34:1–10
Psalm 42

Psalm 55

Psalm 73

Psalm 77

Psalm 84

Psalm 91

FURTHER READING

The Bumps Are What You Climb on: Encouragement for Difficult Days by Warren W. Wiersbe (Baker Book House, 1982)

Comfort in Times of Sorrow by Roger Carswell (10Publishing, 2014)

A Grief Observed by C.S. Lewis (Harper Collins, 1961)

If I Were God I'd End All the Pain by John Dickson (Matthias Media, 2019)

The Problem of Pain by C.S. Lewis (Harper Collins, 1940)

These Strange Ashes by Elizabeth Elliot (OM Publishing, 1998)

When Heaven Is Silent by Ronald Dunn (Word, 1994)

When Life Falls Apart by Warren W. Wiersbe (Spire, 2001)

Where Is God in a Coronavirus World? by John Lennox (the Good Book Company, 2020)

Why Doesn't God Stop the Trouble? by Roger Carswell (Christian Focus/10Publishing, 2010)

Why Me? by Roger Carswell (10Publishing, 2016)

Why Us?: When Bad Things Happen to God's People by Warren W. Wiersbe, (Revel, 1984)

ENDNOTES

INTRODUCTION: LOOKING FOR GOD IN A MESSED-UP WORLD

1. 5 million people died in the Antonine Plague
    of 165–180 AD. In 541–542, between 30 and 50
    million people died during the Plague of Justinian.
    200 million died in the Black Death (Bubonic
    Plague) of 1347–1351, which wiped out 30–50%
    of Europe's population. The plague originated
    in rats and spread to humans via infected fleas.
    It took 200 years for the continent's population
    to recover. 56 million people died in the 1520
    smallpox epidemic, which killed 90% of the native
    American population. In Europe during the 1800s,
    an estimated 400,000 people were being killed
    annually by smallpox. The first-ever vaccine was
    made to ward off smallpox. In 1918–1919, 40–50
    million people died of Spanish flu. Since 1981, an
    estimated 25–35 million people have died of HIV/
    AIDS. The World Health Organisation officially
    declared Covid-19 a pandemic on 11 May 2020.

1. LIVING WITH QUESTIONS

1. Jean-Dominique Bauby, The Diving-Bell and the Butterfly (Fourth Estate, 1997).

2. Ivan Noble, Like a Hole in the Head (Hodder & Stoughton, 2005).

3. Jean-Dominique Bauby, The Diving-Bell and the Butterfly (Fourth Estate, 1997).

4. Ibid.

5. Thornton Wilder, The Bridge of Luis Rey (Penguin, 1927).

6. Ibid.

7. This earthquake happened on 22 February 2011.

8. This massacre occurred on 15 March 2019.

9. Isaiah 52–53.

10. Deuteronomy 4:20; Job 23:10; Psalm 66:10; Isaiah 48:10; Jeremiah 6:29–30; Jeremiah 9:7; Ezekiel 22:18–22; Zechariah 13:8–9; Malachi 3:2–3; 1 Peter 4:12.

11. Job 9:17; 30:22; Psalm 42:7; 66:12; Jonah 2:3; Mark 4:39.

12. Job 16:14; 19:11–12; Lamentations 2:4–5; 2 Timothy 2:3; 1 Corinthians 16:13.

13. Jeremiah 4:31; Matthew 24:8; 1 Thessalonians 5:3.

14. Amos 9:9; Matthew 3:12; Luke 22:31.

15. Jeremiah 12:5.

16. Job 9:16, 29; 13:3.

17. Isaiah 55:8.

2. LOOKING FOR ANSWERS

1. Elie Wiesel, Night (Penguin, 1981).

2. Quote according to Lactanius in A Treatise on the Anger of God.

3. Thomas Hardy, 'Nature's Questioning' (1898).

4. Richard Dawkins, River Out of Eden (Basic Books, 1995).

5. Sir Alec Guinness, Blessings in Disguise (Penguin, 1985).

6. There is substantial evidence to substantiate the belief that the Bible is the word of God and Jesus the Son of God. The fulfilled prophesies of the Bible, as well as its unity in ideas, doctrines and even use of words, point to this collection of sixty-six books being inspired by One who is beyond time – knowing the past, present and future. The historical evidence of the resurrection of Jesus, three days after His crucifixion, provides every reason for believing that Jesus had power over death and was trustworthy in His claim to be God, doing what only God can do. See Appendix 2 for a list of further reading on these issues.

7. Romans 11:33.

8. 1 John 4:8.

9.   Psalm 89:14.

10. Revelation 15:3 (NIV).

11. Deuteronomy 29:29 (NIV).

12. Matthew Henry, The Zondervan NIV Matthew Henry Commentary (Zondervan, 1992).

13. Penned by Dora Greenwell, 1821–1882.

14. In a personal interview with the author.

15. Romans 8:28.

16. Warren Wiersbe, Be Patient (Kingsway, 1991).

17. Quote attributed to the American essayist and poet Ralph Waldo Emmerson (1803–1882).

18. Habakkuk 3:17–18 (NIV).

3. THE WORLD AS IT WAS

1.   John Milton, Paradise Lost: Book 8.

2.   Genesis 1:1.

3.   Revelation 13:8 (NIV).

4.   John C. Lennox, Where Is God in a Coronavirus World? (The Good Book Company, 2020).

5.   James 1:13.

6.   Augustine of Hippo (354–430 AD).

7.   www.satchmo.net

8.   Peter Balakian, The Burning Tigris (Harper Collins, 2003).

9.   Ibid.

10.   Ibid.

4. THE WORLD TAKES A TURN

1.   Genesis 3 describes what happened.

2.   Wladyslaw Szpilman, The Pianist (Phoenix, 1999).

3.   O, The Oprah Magazine, 13 October 2009.

4.   The Daily Telegraph, 14 January 2004.

5.   Romans 3:23.

6.   Matthew 22:37.

7.   Cross-examination of Hermann Goering (1) from 'Eighty-Fourth Day, Monday, 3/18/1946, Part 16', in Trial of the Major War Criminals Before the International Military Tribunal. Volume IX. Proceedings: 3/8/1946–3/23/1946 (Nuremberg: IMT, 1947).

8.   Matthew 7:11 (NIV).

9.   Taken from Charles Colson, Who Speaks for God? (Tyndale House, 1994).

10.   Warren Wiersbe, Why Us? (Revel, 1984).

11.   John 9:1–3.

12.   For example, Mark 7:20–23.

CASE STUDY 2

1.   Romans 12:21.

2.   Galatians 4:4 (NIV).

5. THE WORLD IS RESCUED

1.   John 1:1, 14.

2.   700 years before Christ, Isaiah prophesied, 'For unto us a Child is born, unto us a Son is given; and the government will be upon His shoulder. And His name will be called Wonderful, Counsellor, Mighty God, Everlasting Father, Prince of Peace. Of the increase of His government and peace there will be no end' (Isaiah 9:6–7). Even Jesus' birthplace was prophesied 500 years before His birth by Micah: 'But you, Bethlehem Ephrathah, though you are little among the thousands of Judah, yet out of you shall come forth to Me the One to be Ruler in Israel, whose goings forth are from of old, from everlasting' (Micah 5:2). There are numerous other prophesies concerning the birth, life, death, rising again and influence of Jesus, for instance: Genesis 3:15; 21:12; 49:10; Isaiah 7:14; 8:14; 9:1–2; 35:5–6; 52:14; 53; Psalm 22.

3.   Dorothy Sayers in the essay 'The Greatest Drama Ever Staged' published in The Poetry of Search and the Poetry of Statement (now out of print).

4.   Mark 15:14.

5.   Matthew 27:19 (NIV).

6.   Matthew 27:22–23 (NIV).

7. Matthew 27:25.

8. Matthew 27:26.

9. For example, Matthew 20:18–19, 28; 21:42; John 10:17–18.

10. Galatians 1:4

11. Titus 2:11, 13–14.

12. The Daily Telegraph, 19 December 2003.

13. Luke 23:34 (NIV).

14. Luke 23:46.

15. Mark 15:34 (NIV).

16. 2 Corinthians 5:21.

17. Quoted in Charles Colson, Who Speaks for God? (Crossway, 1995).

18. 1 John 1:7 and 9.

19. John 20:6–7.

20. This phrase is taken from a famous misquote of Bishop David Jenkins, previously Bishop of Durham, 1984–1994.

21. See, for instance: Professor Sir J.N.D. Anderson, Christianity, the Witness of History (Tyndale Press, 1970); Professor F.F. Bruce, The New Testament Documents: Are They reliable? (IVP, 1959); or Roger Carswell, Why I Believe? (10Publishing, 2019).

22. John 14:6.

CASE STUDY 3

1. Romans 8:28 (NIV).

2. Jeremiah 29:13.

3. Revelation 21:6 (NIV).

4. Revelation 21:4.

5. Matthew 11:28–30

6. THE WORLD AS IT WILL BE

1. Revelation 21:1–8.

2. Rodney Hartman, Ali: The Life of Ali Bacher (Penguin, 2004).

3. Romans 6:23.

4. Matthew 23:37 (NIV).

5. John 14:6.

6. Revelation 20:11–15 (NIV).

7. Harold S. Kushner, When Bad Things Happen to Good People (Random House, 1981).

8. The Martyrdom of St Polycarp, Bishop of Smyrna, as recorded in the letter of the Church of Smyrna to the Church of Philomelium, The Apostolic Fathers: Ante-Nicene Library (T & T Clark).

9. Psalm 73:25.

10. Psalm 73:28.

CASE STUDY 4

1. John 11: 25–26.

2. Deuteronomy 31:8.

7. CHANGE

1. Leo Tolstoy, A Confession and What I Believe (Oxford University Press, 1921).

2. 2 Corinthians 5:17.

3. Ken Abraham and Lisa Beamer, Let's Roll! (Tyndale House, 2005).

4. Revelation 21:3–4 (NIV).

8. COMFORT

1. 1 Peter 5:7.

2. Luke 22:44.

3. Luke 24:15–16.

4. Luke 24:32 (NIV).

5. Luke 24:46–47.

6. 1 Thessalonians 4:13 (NIV).

7. Psalm 42:5.

8. Psalm 42:8.

9. Acts 16:25.

10. The Spafford story, and the hymn in full, can

be found at https://en.wikipedia.org/wiki/
Horatio_Spafford

11. John 11:25–26.

9. FORGIVENESS

1. C.S. Lewis, Mere Christianity (Harper Collins, 1952).

2. This story can be found in Matthew 18:21–35.

3. Luke 17:3–4.

4. Matthew 5:7.

5. Luke 11:4 (NIV).

6. Luke 23:34 (NIV).

7. Ephesians 4:32 (NIV).

8. Taken from Hitler's Obersalzberg Speech to his Wehrmacht commanders.

9. The booklet 'Armenian Experts in the Art of Dying' by Rev. Sisag Manoogian. Sisag Manoogian's biography, Out of the Ark, is available as an ebook through www.10ofthose.com

10. Genesis 50:20 (NIV).

10. COMPASSION

1. Story told by Lindsay Brown, General Secretary of IFES, at the IFES Europe & Eurasia 'Get Connected' conference in Hungary, Easter 2004.

2. Micah 6:8.

3. Mark 6:34 (NIV).

4. 1 John 3:17–18 (NIV).

5. Luke 4:18 (NIV), where Jesus is quoting from Isaiah 61:1–2.

6. Nelson Mandela, Long Walk to Freedom (Little Brown & Co, 1995).

11. ACCEPTANCE

1. www.janisian.com/lyrics

2. Matthew 6:25–34 (NIV).

3. Psalm 55:22.

4. In a letter dated 29 April 1959.

5. Isaiah 40:28–31 (NIV).

6. John 13:7 (NIV).

7. In a talk entitled 'When you get to the end of your rope', delivered at the Association of Evangelists' Conference, England.

8. Acts 10:38.

9. 3 John 2 (NIV).

10. Anglican Book of Common Prayer.

CONCLUSION: FINDING GOD IN A MESSED-UP WORLD

1. Luke 13:1–5 (NIV).

2. John 9:3 (NIV).

3. 2 Chronicles 33:1–17.

4. Taken from a sermon delivered by Chaplain Carey Cash at the US Naval Academy Chapel, 30 March 2014.

5. Matthew 11:28 (NIV).

6. John 3:16.

7. The grave of Jane Baillie Welsh can be found in the Old Abbey Kirk graveyard, in Haddington, East Lothian, Scotland.

8. Romans 10:13 (NIV).

APPENDIX 1 – DEPRESSION: A PERSONAL POINT OF VIEW

1. 1 Timothy 2:8 (NIV).

2. I particularly valued 'The Book of Psalms' produced by Timothy Botts – it is the Book of Psalms but includes highlighted verses painted with his calligraphy.

3. Psalm 42:5.

4. This is prophesied in Isaiah 53:3.

5. Isaiah 45:3.